Becky Goldsmith and Linda Jenkins

Wool Appliqué

the Piece O' Cake Way

12 Cheerful Projects
Mix Wool with Cotton & Linen

C&T PUBLISHING

Publisher: Amy Marson

Creative Director: Gailen Runge

Art Director: Kristy Zacharias

Editor: Lynn Koolish

Technical Editors: Alison M. Schmidt and Debbie Rodgers

Cover/Book Designer: April Mostek

Page Layout Artist: Casey Dukes

Production Coordinators: Zinnia Heinzmann and Rue Flaherty

Production Editor: Katie Van Amburg

Illustrators: Becky Goldsmith and Rue Flaherty

Photo Assistant: Mary Peyton Peppo

Photography by Diane Pedersen, unless otherwise noted

Published by C&T Publishing, Inc., P.O. Box 1456, Lafayette, CA 94549

Library of Congress Cataloging-in-Publication Data

Goldsmith, Becky, 1956-

Wool appliqué the Piece O' Cake way : 12 cheerful projects - mix wool with cotton & linen / Becky Goldsmith and Linda Jenkins.

pages cm

ISBN 978-1-61745-047-1 (soft cover)

1. Appliqué--Patterns. 2. Quilting. I. Jenkins, Linda, 1943- II. Piece O'Cake Designs. III. Title.

TT779.G66 2015

746.44'5--dc23

2014047453

Printed in China

10 9 8 7 6 5 4 3 2 1

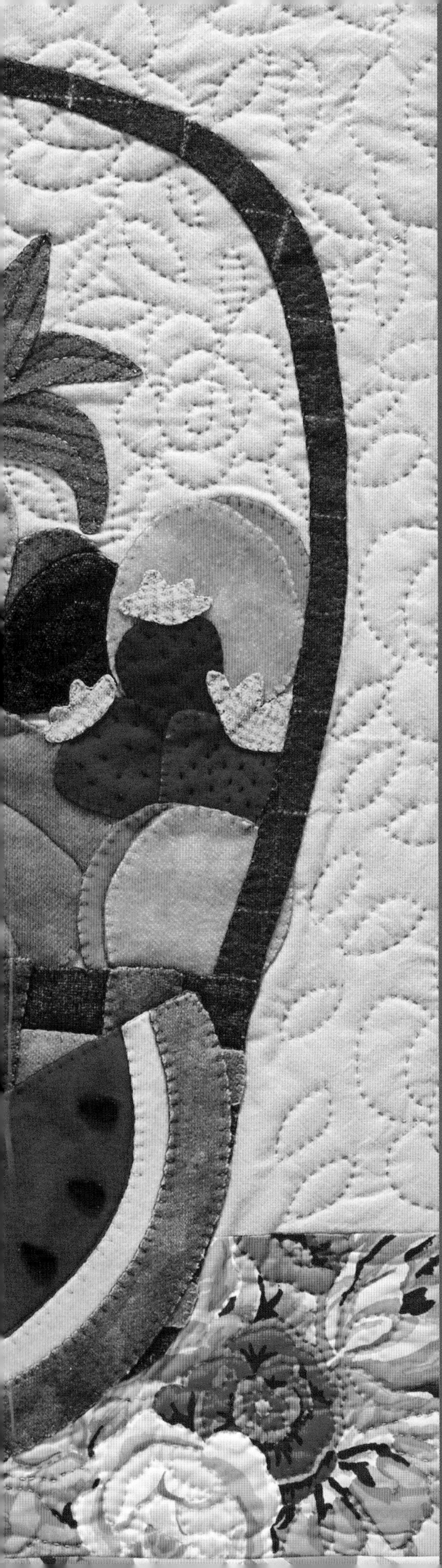

Contents

Acknowledgments

The fine folks at C&T have been very good to us. First, Todd Hensley, CEO, welcomed us with open arms. Amy Marson, publisher, is always there to support us. Lynn Koolish, our editor, has helped to make each and every book of ours shine. Diane Pedersen takes photos that are sharp and clear and lovely. We appreciate the help they have all given to us.

It would be nice to be perfect, but we aren't, so we are very grateful to Alison Schmidt, our technical editor, who makes sure we get the details right. Rue Flaherty and Zinnia Heinzmann, the production coordinators, and Katie Van Amburg, the production editor, kept everything in this complicated book on track. April Mostek, this book's designer, worked her magic to give this book its distinctive appearance. We thank you all for your excellent efforts.

We want to also thank Phyliss Meiring from ***in the Patch designs***. She shared her knowledge with us *and* she dyed Christmas-red wool especially for us. That color, and more, can be found at ***in the Patch designs***. We loved working with her wool.

Dedication

It is easy to find your quilting niche and it is tempting to stay there. It can be hard to make yourself try something new and different. We dedicate this book to those who love to try something new, who love learning new techniques and ways to accomplish new things.

There is so much fun and reward that comes from making something totally different from what you have done before. If you have never worked with felted wool, we encourage you to give it a try. We think you will love it.

Linda and Becky

Introduction

Linda started appliquéing with felted wool a few years ago, and this book was her idea. It makes perfect sense that she should be the one to introduce you to what you'll find as you turn the pages. . . .

Linda's batik and felted wool *Simply Delicious* quilt

I began to purchase small pieces of felted wool some time ago. At the time I wasn't sure how I was going to use it, but the texture and colors in the cloth drew me in.

Not having any idea what I would do with my wool was actually a good thing. It allowed me to think about how to use wool in a new way. I began to explore combining felted wool with other fabrics. The results were amazing.

My first project was a quilt made from our Simply Delicious ePattern. I sewed felted wool appliqué to batik backgrounds. Wow. I loved it.

As I stitched, I realized that appliquéing felted wool is different from appliquéing cotton, and that is why I wanted to write this book. In it, you will find tips and techniques that make appliquéing felted wool a breeze.

I hope you have as much fun as I do as you stitch with felted wool.

Happy stitching,

Linda

Getting Started

Basic Supplies

A. Cotton and linen fabric: Look for 100% cotton, 100% linen, and cotton/linen blend fabrics. Always prewash cottons and linens.

B. Felted wool fabric: The wool fabrics used in these quilts are 100% felted wool (not wool felt). Refer to Felted Wool or Wool Felt? (page 10).

Design wall: This is a must-have tool. We each have a design wall made from 1″ thick insulation foam, available in 4′ × 8′ sheets from a home improvement store. Use as many sheets as necessary to cover your wall space. The foam is easy to cut. It can be attached to the wall with sheetrock screws and then covered with white flannel or batting. You can use a portable design wall if that suits your needs better.

Piecing thread: We used Superior MasterPiece 50-weight 3-ply cotton (on the spool) or Aurifil 2-ply 50-weight cotton.

Appliqué thread:

C. Aurifil's wool thread works well when hand appliquéing felted wool. It is a slightly fuzzy, 50% acrylic/50% wool blend thread that is not showy when used with felted wool fabric. You will see the word *lana* on the Aurifil spool. *Lana* means "wool" in Italian.

D. Use Presencia's perle cotton in either a 12 or 16 weight for appliqué stitches with attitude (page 31). This thread can also be used to appliqué felted wool when you want a thread that is more visible with a bit of a sheen on top of the felted wool. It is a good choice for big-stitch hand quilting.

E. We recommend Superior MasterPiece 50-weight 2-ply cotton (available only on bobbins), Aurifil 50-weight cotton, and DMC 50-weight machine embroidery thread for traditional invisible appliqué stitches on cotton and linen fabrics.

Machine quilting thread: Superior's King Tut 40-weight cotton is very nice with felted wool appliqué.

Hand quilting thread: We like Gütterman's cotton hand quilting thread. Perle cotton size 12 or 16 is nice when you want bigger, more visible stitches.

F. Pins: Use ⅝″ appliqué pins to pin appliqué pieces in place—we like the Essential Appliqué Pins from Piece O' Cake Designs. Use fine, long pins for piecing.

G. Needles: For hand appliqué with thicker threads, use a bigger needle. A Richard Hemming & Son 7 or 9 sharp works well, as does Bohin's 9 crewel needle.

When sewing a traditional appliqué invisible stitch with finer thread, use a smaller needle. Clover's 12 Black Gold sharp is nice. If you like a longer needle, try a size 11 Hemming & Son milliners (or straw) needle.

In both cases, there are many good needles; find the one that fits *your* hand.

H. Needle threader: The Quilter's Threaders are hand-held threaders that are helpful with thicker threads and larger needles.

I. Scissors: Good scissors are a joy to use. Use a scissor with smooth blades on felted wool. A scissor with a serrated blade works well with cotton and linen. Small to medium-size, sharp scissors are better for precise cutting.

Rotary cutter, mat, and acrylic ruler: When trimming blocks to size and cutting borders, rotary cutting tools will give you the best results.

J. Pencils: To draw around templates onto cotton or linen fabric, use a General's Charcoal white pencil, or a mechanical chalk pencil that holds a 9 mm refill. We use either white or gray chalk depending on the color and value of the fabric.

K. Permanent markers: To make the positioning overlay for appliqué, a black Sharpie Ultra Fine Point permanent marker works well on vinyl.

Clear or frosted vinyl: Use a clear or frosted flexible, medium-weight vinyl to make the positioning overlay. If the vinyl you buy comes with tissue paper, keep the tissue paper for storage. If your quilt shop does not have vinyl, look for it in online or in stores that carry upholstery fabric.

You will also need clear vinyl if you make the Strawberry Zip Bag (page 51).

L. Clear, single-sided, heavyweight self-laminating sheets: Use them to make templates. We recommend the Piece O' Cake Essential Self-Adhesive Laminating Sheets (see Resources, page 79). You can find self-laminating sheets at pieceocake.com, at most office supply stores, at some warehouse markets, or online. Buy the single-sided sheets, not the pouches. If you can't find laminating sheets, you can use clear contact paper.

M. Sandpaper board: When tracing around templates onto fabric, place the fabric on the sandpaper side of the board. Then place the template on the fabric. You'll love the way the sandpaper holds the fabric in place when you trace. We recommend the Piece O' Cake Essential Sandboard.

Wooden toothpick: Use a round, wooden toothpick when hand appliquéing cotton and linen fabrics to help turn under the turn-under allowance at points and curves. Wood has a texture that grabs and holds the fabric.

N. Fusible web: We use SoftFuse to hold felted wool appliqué shapes to the block for stitching. It is available in 8″ × 9″ sheets and on an 18″-wide roll. Follow the manufacturer's instructions for this or any fusible that you use.

If you choose to fuse the cotton and linen appliqué pieces, use the product that works best for you. Always follow the manufacturer's instructions. It's a good idea to test the fusible web on the fabric you will be using.

Spray starch: Use spray starch to add body to lighter background fabrics such as vintage cotton and some linen.

Nonstick appliqué pressing sheet: Always press felted wool with a pressing sheet because ironing directly onto felted wool can leave scorch marks. A nonstick pressing sheet will protect the iron and ironing board when you are using fusible web. Additionally, a nonstick pressing sheet really does help the fusible web to adhere better.

Quick Yo-Yo Maker (Small) by Clover: Used to make the 1¼″-diameter yo-yos for the *Yo-Yo Garden Foot Warmer* (page 44) and *Yo-Yo Basket* (page 72). Refer to the instructions on the package and/or online.

Wonder Clips by Clover: These clips are wonderful to use for their intended purpose (holding fabric layers together without pins), but they also come in very handy if you use them as binding clips for projects like the Strawberry Zip Bag (page 51).

1″ bias tape maker: You feed a bias strip through this little gizmo and it comes out the other side with the raw edges folded into the center of the strip, ready to press as you go. This is a handy tool if you are making the Strawberry Zip Bag (page 51).

A good work light: Choose a lamp that gives off a bright, natural light. Sewing is so much easier when you can see what you are doing.

Polyester stuffing for the Leafy Pillows (page 62)

Stuffing for the Strawberry Pincushions (page 56): Use wool, cotton, polyester, or crushed pecan shell lizard litter. Lizard litter can be found at some pet supply stores or online.

Batting: We use cotton batting. There are several good batts on the market. It is a good idea to do some research to find the batt that suits you best. Our current favorite is Quilters Dream Select.

Quilting gloves: Quilting gloves make it easier to hold onto the quilt during machine quilting. Machingers brand is our favorite.

Sewing machine: Successful machine piecing and quilting requires the best sewing machine and table that you can afford. For piecing, we use a Bernina. For machine quilting we use the Sweet Sixteen by Handi Quilter.

Appliqué Caddy

We also designed the Quilter's Appliqué Caddy, which we love to use to keep our appliqué pieces in. You can get it at your local quilt shop or online.

About Fabric Requirements

Cotton fabric is usually 40″–42″ wide off the bolt. Linen can be wider than 40″, but it isn't always wider than that. To be safe, all fabric requirements are based on a 40″ width.

Use the fabric requirements for each quilt as a guide, but remember that yardage amounts can vary depending on how you cut the fabric. The measurements in this book allow for some fabric shrinkage and minor errors in cutting.

Felted Wool

Felted wool comes in a variety of sizes. These are the most common:

Charm: 5″ × 5″

Chubby: 16″ × 16″

Chunk: 9″ × 10″

Commercial Chubby: 18″ × 18″

You can buy felted wool yardage off the bolt from some companies.

Borders

This book's cutting instructions are mathematically correct. However, variations in the finished size of the quilt top can result from slight differences in seam allowances. You should *always* measure your quilt before adding borders. When measuring, be sure to measure through the middle of the quilt top, not at the outer edges, which can stretch. Adjust the size of the borders if necessary.

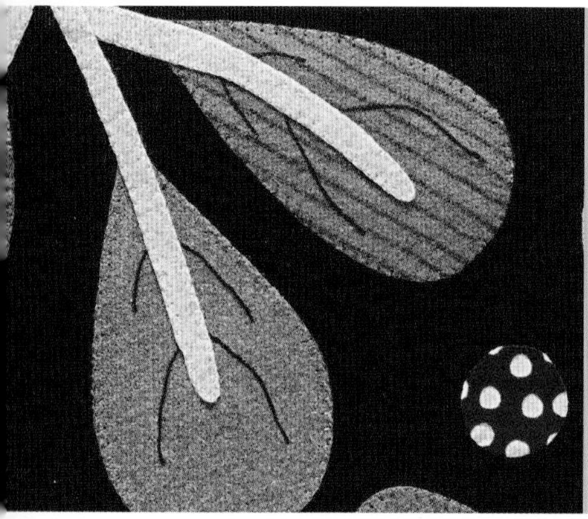

Felted Wool, Cotton, and Linen

Felted wool is thick and fuzzy; cotton is smooth and often patterned; linen is heavier than cotton and a little bit coarser. These three types of fabric look (and feel) different from each other and you can see that difference at a glance.

Quilts are built on the contrast between things that are different. It is the difference between the elements in the design that makes some areas more (or less) visible. It is contrast that marks the difference between one shape and another, between foreground and background, between smooth and fuzzy, between thick and thin fabrics.

It is the contrast between these three very different kinds of cloth that makes them perfect companions.

Felted Wool or Wool Felt?

Felted wool and wool felt are two different kinds of cloth.

Felted wool is thick and fuzzy, which gives it a distinct physical and visual texture. These two attributes also affect the color of wool. The colors are more nuanced whether the felted wool is a solid, plaid, or stripe.

You can see the woven threads in the cloth, even after it has been felted. The horizontal and vertical threads catch the light differently. The threads are thick enough, and dense enough, to cast shadows in the cloth. This adds to the feeling of thickness and depth. Even a solid color appears to be a bit more than just "solid."

The top, fuzzy layer of the cloth keeps felted wool from ever appearing to be shiny. It also acts like a fine layer of fog, adding to the soft visual texture.

Felted wool begins with a woven cloth made from 100% wool. The cloth may come off the bolt, from old clothes, or from some other source. Simply stated, the cloth becomes felt when it is washed in hot water and dried in a hot dryer—a process called *fulling*. This causes the wool fibers to shrink, pulling them together to make a thicker, felted wool cloth.

Felted Knits

If you've ever washed and dried a 100% wool sweater, you know that knit fabric can also be felted or fulled. This type of felted wool feels different from felted wool that is made from a woven cloth. It can be thicker and denser, depending on the weight of the yarn that was used to make the cloth.

Felted knit is not the kind of felted wool that you would typically find in a quilt shop, and it is not one that we used in these quilts. But you could use it if you wanted to.

Felted wool is made from woven wool cloth.

Felted wool rarely frays at the edges during stitching. When it does, it is usually because the wool has not been felted enough.

Wool Felt

Wool felt is made from loose wool fibers that are placed together in layers that run alternately lengthwise and crosswise. The bed of layers is wetted and a little soap is added. The fibers are then rubbed together—this process is called "felting." The more the fibers are agitated, the tighter the felt will be.

At the end of the process the soap is rinsed away with cool water. The felt is pressed or squeezed to remove excess water, and then is it laid flat to dry.

Dense, tight wool felt has a flat appearance, and it can be a little stiff. Soft wool felt was more gently agitated, making it a looser cloth. The fibers can sometimes pull apart, and it has a softer edge. In both cases, we find that wool felt is not what we want to use in hand appliqué.

Wool felt is made from loose wool fibers that are compressed to form flat, dense cloth. We prefer felted wool.

Cotton comes in beautiful prints and solids that look great with felted wool.

Cotton

You are a quilter. You know that cotton cloth is physically smooth and that it is thinner than felted wool. You also know that cotton comes in almost any color or pattern imaginable. However, because cotton is so different from felted wool, you might not have thought of using them together in appliqué.

Cotton appliqué shapes sparkle when combined with felted wool appliqué. This is especially true of printed cotton cloth. The patterns and colors on the cotton add excitement to mostly solid felted wools. Each kind of fabric enhances the other.

Cotton is lovely when used as a background underneath felted wool appliqué shapes. The thicker felted wool sits higher on it than do appliqué shapes cut from cotton, which adds real depth to the design.

Linen

Linen is a fabric that is not used as often to make quilts. Instead, linen has traditionally been used in the home: on the bed or as dish towels, napkins, tablecloths, and so on. Linen is also used to make garments, especially those that might be worn in hot, humid weather.

While there are very finely woven linen fabrics, the linen that works best with felted wool is somewhat heavier and coarser than quilting cottons.

Linen is heavier than cotton, with pronounced texture.

Linen is prone to wrinkling. That's more of a problem in a garment than it is in a quilt. Press linen fabric before you begin sewing with it. Press the blocks again before you quilt them.

To be honest, it can be hard to find linen on the bolt in a quilt shop. When we find an interesting piece of linen, we buy it because you never know when you might find more. We like linen/cotton blends. They are heavier than cotton and lighter than linen but still have a linenlike texture that is very nice with felted wool.

In all cases, prewash linen, because it will shrink. This will pull the fibers together, making the fabric easier to work with. Refer to Cotton and Linen Fabric Preparation (page 15).

Preparing to Stitch

Felted Wool Preparation

Prewash cotton and linen fabrics—they often shrink and the colors can bleed. Felted wool has already been shrunk so you don't need to worry about shrinking.

If you believe that your felted wool project will never need to be washed, don't prewash the wool. If your wool fabric is wrinkled, press it with a hot iron and a nonstick pressing sheet.

If you plan to wash your project, you need to check the felted wool for colorfastness. Wet the felted wool and steam press with a light-colored cloth underneath. If the color bleeds, then wash the felted wool using Synthrapol, Retayne, or Color Catcher sheets made by Shout.

Please note that it is possible that the felted wool may shrink a bit more when washed or pressed with steam.

Always Use Fusible Web for Felted Wool Appliqué

Fusible web serves two functions in appliqué with felted wool: it holds the felted wool appliqué pieces in place as you stitch and it adds needed body to the felted wool. SoftFuse paper-backed fusible web is our choice for fusing felted wool appliqué pieces. It is so light that you can hardly feel it on the back of the felted wool. Other fusible webs can be too thick, making the appliqué stiff and hard to needle.

Use a nonstick pressing sheet when applying the fusible to the felted wool. We're not entirely sure why it makes the fusible web adhere better—maybe it diffuses and intensifies the heat of the iron—but it does help. Always follow the manufacturer's fusing instructions. It's a good idea to test the fusible web on the fabric you will be using.

Should the fusible come loose as you stitch, place pins in a few key spots to hold the appliqué in place. Add more pins if they are needed.

Fuse felted wool appliqué pieces in place. Supplement with pins as needed.

There is no turn-under allowance on felted wool appliqué shapes. However, you do need ½″ of extra fabric in those places where one appliqué shape falls underneath another one. Be sure to include that seam allowance on the fusible web when you trace the shapes.

The Best Threads to Use with Felted Wool

Aurifil's wool thread is 50% acrylic and 50% wool. The acrylic fibers give the thread strength and cut down on the fuzziness that you'll find in many 100% wool threads. You will see the word *lana* on the Aurifil spool. *Lana* means "wool" in Italian.

Wool thread is fuzzy in the same way that felted wool is fuzzy. It nestles against the fabric and blends well with it.

Presencia's perle cotton is a thicker, more tightly twisted thread with a bit more sheen than Aurifil's wool thread. Perle cotton size 12 is a bit thicker than size 16, but both of them are thicker than the Aurifil's wool. This thickness adds dimension to the stitches on felted wool.

The appliqué stitches with attitude, sewn on cotton appliqué fabric, are made with perle cotton (see Appliqué with Attitude on Cotton, page 31). This thread is also nice to use for big-stitch hand quilting.

In all cases, you can choose to match the thread color to the fabric or use a contrasting color to highlight shapes.

Aurifil's wool thread

Presencia's Finca Perlé Cotton thread sizes 12 and 16. The 2 weights look the same at a glance so be sure to check the label for the weight you want.

Cotton and Linen Fabric Preparation

If you haven't already, please consider washing and drying (called prewashing) your cotton and linen fabric before using it. Why?

- Prewash cotton and linen fabric to remove excess dye and other chemicals, such as insecticides, in the cloth. These chemicals cause an allergic reaction in some people.
- Most cotton fabrics will shrink when washed and dried. Different fabrics shrink at different rates; it is better if the fabric has been shrunk to size *before* it has been sewn into the quilt.
- Fabric off the bolt has a finish that makes it feel a little slick. Washing removes this finish. The fabric will fuse better after these finishes are washed away.
- In both piecing and appliqué, it is much easier to sew together fabrics that are not sliding against each other.
- The seam allowances will fray less if you prewash and dry the fabric. Frayed edges can be hard to work with.

Spray Starch

Felted wool is both heavier and thicker than woven cotton and linen fabrics are. You may need to add spray starch to background fabrics that seem light. This is especially true for vintage cottons that may have already been subjected to wear and tear.

Design and Audition

The best way to know that the colors you have chosen are going to work together is to audition them on your design wall *before* you begin sewing.

Each fabric is auditioning for its role in the quilt. Some fabrics will be perfect. Others will not make the cut. You really don't know until you see them in place on the wall. *You can't fake the audition.* Sticking some fat quarters on the wall and hoping for the best doesn't work.

As you audition your fabric, remember that every color is affected by the color (or colors) next to it. As you make the quilt, you need to be constantly aware of this and pay attention to the way the fabrics are reacting to each other on the design wall.

When we make an appliqué quilt, we cut and place every piece in position on the design wall before ever taking a stitch. By doing this, we *know* that the quilt is going to be wonderful before we put all those stitches into it.

Begin by placing the backgrounds on the design wall. If you are going to piece the backgrounds, put as much as you can on the design wall.

Starting with the first block, trace and cut out the appliqué pieces. Begin with whatever piece seems like the most obvious choice to you. Add the necessary turn-under allowances and cut carefully so that if you like the way an appliqué piece looks, you won't have to recut it.

No Peeling Yet

Leave the paper backing on the felted wool appliqué pieces during the design phase. It is handy to have the numbers on the paper backing to refer to when you are fusing the pieces to the block. However, because the paper is slick, you will need to pin the appliqué pieces in place on the design wall. Use short pins that don't interfere with the overlay.

Continue cutting and placing shapes until everything is on the wall. Stand back and really look at the quilt. Is it the way you want it to be? If you aren't sure, take a photo. Seeing the quilt in the camera or on the computer screen does help you to see what's really there. Once you are happy, you are ready to make the quilt.

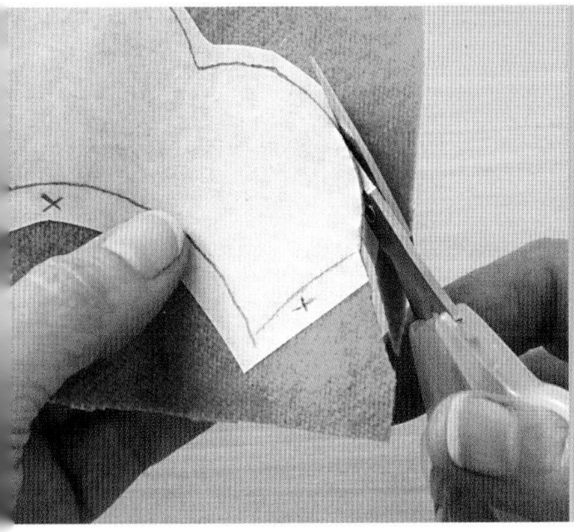

General Appliqué Instructions

For a more complete description of all of our appliqué techniques, refer to our book The Best-Ever Appliqué Sampler *and the DVD* Becky Goldsmith and Linda Jenkins Teach You to Appliqué the Piece O' Cake Way.

Preparing Cotton and Linen Backgrounds

Always cut the background fabric larger than the size it will be when it is pieced into the quilt. The outer edges of the block can stretch and fray as you handle it while stitching. The appliqué can shift during stitching and cause the block to shrink slightly. We add 2″ in both directions to the finished size of the block in our cutting instructions.

1. Press each background block in half vertically and horizontally. This establishes a center grid in the background that will line up with the center grid on the positioning overlay (see Making the Positioning Overlay, page 22).
2. Use a pencil or permanent marker to draw a ¼″-long mark on each end of the pressed-in grid lines, at the edges of the block. *Be sure not to make the lines too long or they will show on the block.* These lines will make it easier to correctly position the overlay.
3. Use a pencil or permanent marker to draw a little X in *the upper right-hand corner* of the block background near the outer edge. This X will be in the same corner as an X that you will draw on the overlay. *Be sure to mark the X near the edge so it won't show on the finished block.*

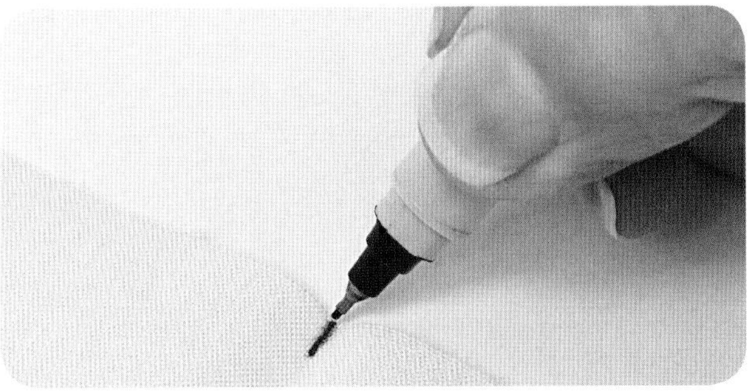

Mark ends of pressed lines.

Draw small X in upper right corner of background.

Making the Appliqué Templates

Each appliqué shape requires a template, and we have a unique way to make templates that is both easy and accurate. Use clear, single-sided, heavyweight self-laminating sheets to make templates. We recommend the Piece O' Cake Essential Self-Laminating sheets. They are just a little heavier than the the laminate available at most office supply stores. The extra thickness makes them easier to use. You can find them at your local quilt shop or online at pieceocake.com. Also look for self-adhesive laminate sheets at an office supply store.

1. Use a photocopier to make 2 or 3 copies of each block. Always compare the copies with the original to be sure they are the same size.

2. Cut out the appliqué shapes from these copies. Group them when you can—it saves on the laminate. Leave a little paper allowance around each shape or group. Where a shape overlaps another, cut the top shape and the bottom shape from 2 different copies.

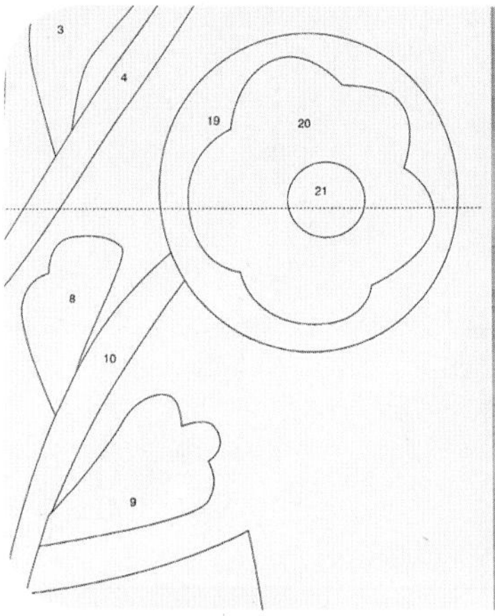

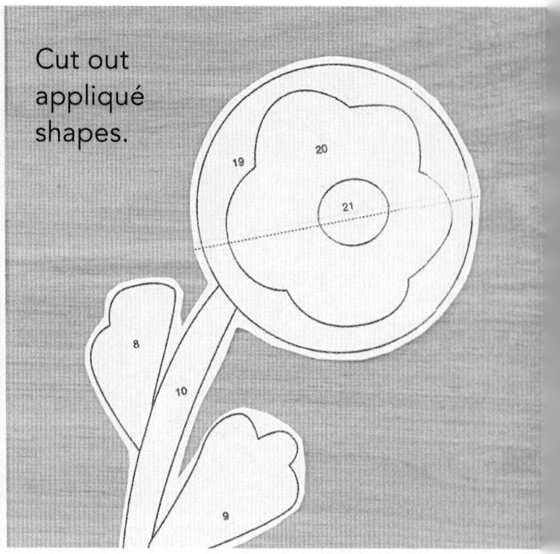

Cut out appliqué shapes.

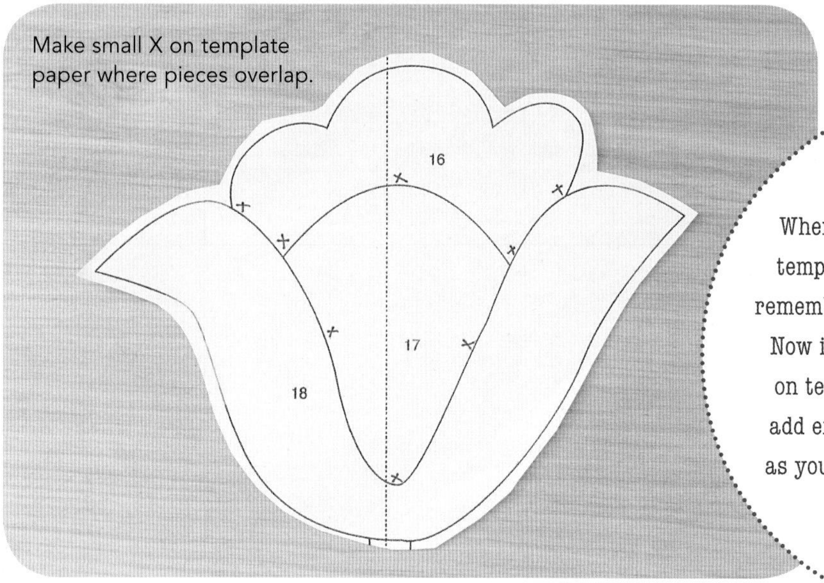

Make small X on template paper where pieces overlap.

Mark the Overlap

When you are looking at individual templates as you work, it is hard to remember exactly where pieces overlap. Now is a good time to make a little X on templates where you will need to add extra seam allowance. That way, as you trace onto the fusible web, you will be alerted.

3. Place a self-laminating sheet shiny side down on the table. Peel off the paper backing, leaving the sticky side of the sheet facing up.

4. Felted wool appliqué shapes are always fused to the block (see Always Use Fusible Web for Felted Wool Appliqué, page 14). For shapes that will be fused, place the templates *blank side down* on the self-laminating sheet.

   For appliqué shapes that will be sewn using needle-turn appliqué, place the templates *right side down* on the self-laminating sheet. Take care when placing copies onto the laminate so that the paper lies flat, without wrinkles. Use more laminating sheets as necessary.

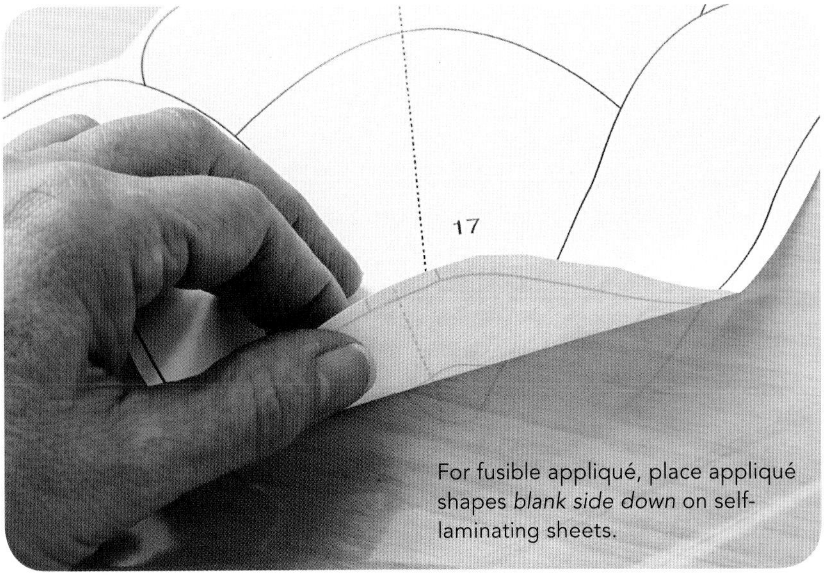

For fusible appliqué, place appliqué shapes *blank side down* on self-laminating sheets.

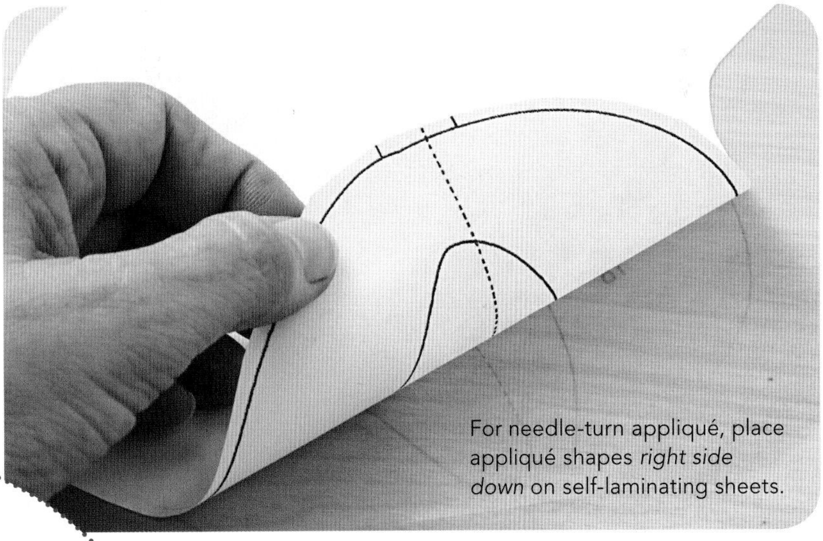

For needle-turn appliqué, place appliqué shapes *right side down* on self-laminating sheets.

What If I Don't Know?

When you make templates, you may not know which shapes will be fused felted wool and which will be needle-turned cotton or linen. If that is the case, make all of the templates for the method that you think will dominate the appliqué. *Then (and this is important) remember to flip them over when you use them for the other method.*

5. Cut out each template. Try to split the drawn line with the scissors—don't cut inside or outside of the line. Keep edges smooth and points sharp.

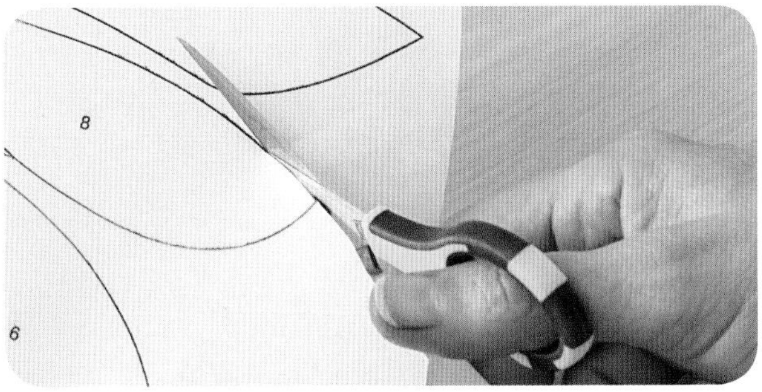

Cut out each template.

Using Templates for Fusible Appliqué

Templates are used right side down on the paper backing of the fusible web for fused appliqué.

1. Place each template face down (right side down) on the paper side of the fusible web. Trace around each template with a fine pencil. Remember to add a ½″ seam allowance on any edge that will be underneath another appliqué shape.

   You can place the templates close together, but leave an ⅛″ buffer around each shape and around the extra that you add where a shape will be under another shape.

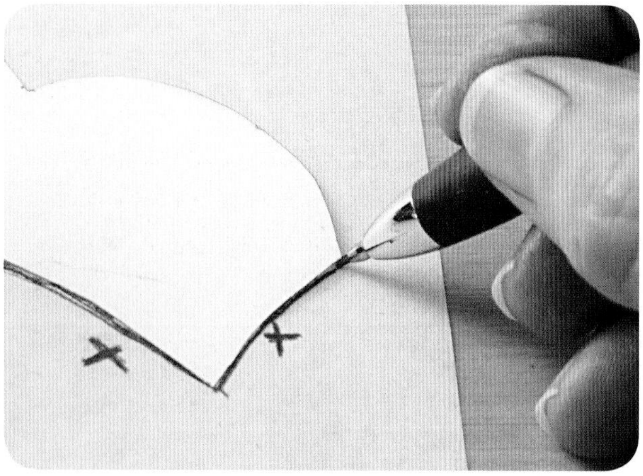

Trace around each template onto paper side of fusible web, adding ½″ seam allowances where needed.

2. Cut out the fusible shapes (cutting both the paper and the fusible web), leaving a scant border of paper around each shape.

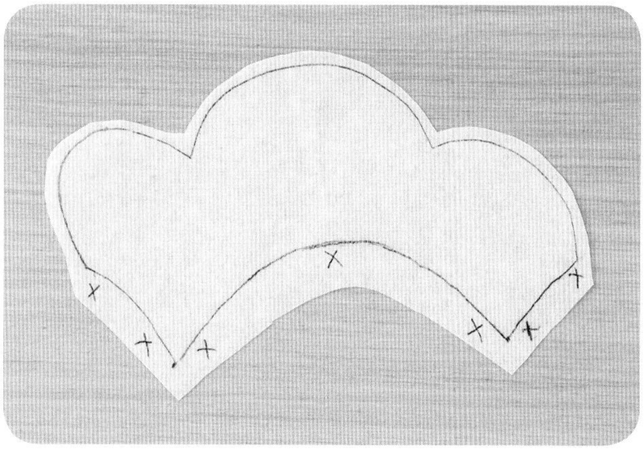

Cut out shapes, leaving edge of paper around each one.

3. Place the appliqué fabric right side down on an ironing board. Place the appropriate fusible shape(s) on the wrong side of the appliqué fabric with the paper backing up.

4. Follow the manufacturer's instructions and iron the fusible web to the *wrong* side of the appliqué fabric. Use a nonstick pressing sheet to protect the iron and ironing board and to prevent felted wool from scorching. The nonstick pressing sheet works better than anything else.

Tip

Use a medium-hot iron and the nonstick pressing sheet when pressing the fusible web to the back of the wool. It may only take 5 seconds. Do not use steam.

Save the Leftovers

You will accumulate little leftover bits of fusible web. Save them in a zip-type bag because they do come in handy.

5. Do not peel off the paper backing. Using sharp scissors, cut out the appliqué pieces just inside the drawn line on the paper backing on finished edges. Do not cut off the ½″ seam allowance where shapes overlap.

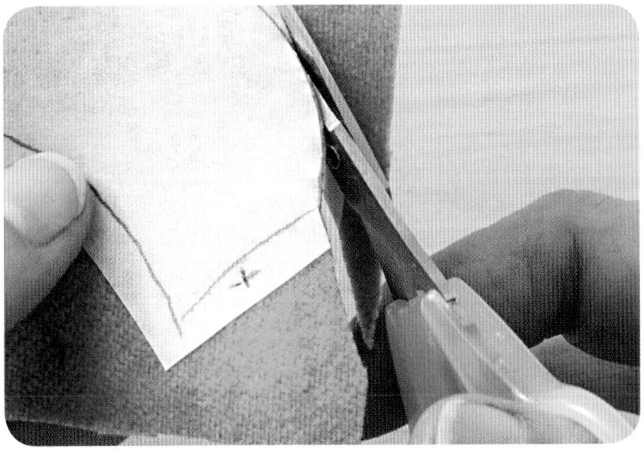

Cut out appliqué pieces on inside of drawn line.

Using the Templates to Appliqué with Attitude

Templates are used right side up on the right side of cotton or linen fabric for needle-turned appliqué.

1. Place the cotton appliqué fabric right side up on a sandpaper board. The sandpaper board will hold the fabric in place while you trace. We think that the Essential Sandboard (see Resources, page 79) is the best sandboard on the market.

2. Place the template right side up on the fabric so that as many edges as possible are on the bias or diagonal grain of the fabric. A bias edge frays less and is easier to turn under than an edge on the straight of grain.

3. Trace around the template. Make a line you can see. Be sure to draw the line right up next to the edge of the template. It won't matter if the line is wide because it gets turned under.

4. Cut out each piece. Add a 3⁄16″ turn-under allowance for *needle-turn hand appliqué*. Add a scant 3⁄8″ allowance to any part of an appliqué piece that will be under another piece.

Place templates with as many edges as possible on diagonal grain and trace around each template.

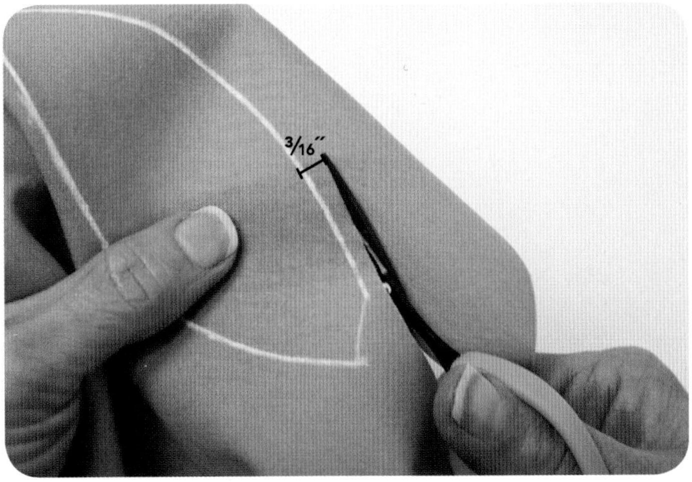

Cut out each piece, adding 3⁄16″ turn-under allowance for hand appliqué.

Making the Positioning Overlay

The positioning overlay is a piece of clear or frosted medium-weight vinyl that is used to position each appliqué piece accurately on the block. The overlay is easy to make and use, and can be used with just about any appliqué method.

1. Cut a piece of the vinyl the finished size of each block and border. If the clear vinyl came with a tissue paper lining, cut the tissue paper as you cut the vinyl. Set the tissue paper aside until you are ready to fold or store the overlay.
2. Tape the pattern onto a table.
3. Tape the vinyl over the pattern. Use a ruler and a black Sharpie Ultra Fine Point permanent marker to draw the pattern's horizontal and vertical centerlines onto the vinyl.
4. Accurately trace all the lines from the pattern onto the vinyl. The numbers on the pattern indicate stitching sequence—include these numbers on the overlay. They also tell you which side of the overlay is the right side.

Accurately trace all lines from pattern onto vinyl.

5. Draw a small X in the upper right-hand corner of the placement overlay. This will help you position the overlay correctly on the block or border.

Draw small X in upper right-hand corner of placement overlay.

6. Fold or roll to store. If the vinyl came with tissue paper, place it over the drawn side of the overlay and fold or roll them together. The tissue paper keeps the lines from transferring from 1 part of the vinyl to another part.

Using the Positioning Overlay

1. If you are fusing the appliqué pieces, place the background right side up on the ironing board.

   If you are positioning pieces for needle-turn appliqué, it is easier to work on top of a sandpaper board. The sandpaper keeps the background from shifting as you position appliqué pieces on the block.

2. Place the overlay right side up on top of the background.

3. Line up the center grid in the background with the center grid of the overlay. Place the X on the overlay in the same corner as the X on the background. Pin the overlay if necessary to keep it from shifting out of position.

4. Place the first appliqué piece under the overlay but on top of the background. It is easy to tell when the appliqué pieces are in position under the overlay. Be sure to place appliqué pieces in numerical order. If you are hand appliquéing and fusing on the same block, you may need to alternate between fusing and hand sewing.

5. For fusible appliqué, remove the paper backing. You can often position 4 or 5 pieces at a time, depending on their position and size. After you have pieces in position, fold the overlay out of the way and fuse them in place using a nonstick pressing sheet.

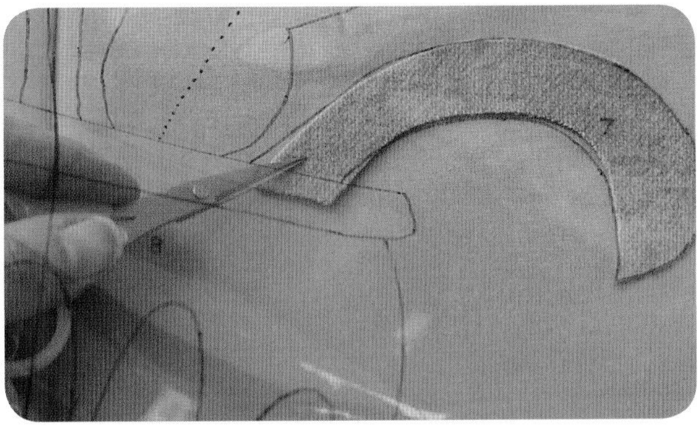

Use overlay to position fusible appliqué pieces.

Tip

Use a medium-hot to hot iron and the nonstick pressing sheet when pressing the wool shapes in place. Press from the top for 15–20 seconds. Let the wool cool and check to see how it is sticking. You may need to flip the block over and, using the pressing sheet, press the back side of the wool appliqué for 5 seconds.

Do not use steam. Do not overpress.

6. Before placing hand appliqué pieces with turn-under allowances on the block, finger-press the turn-under allowance (see Finger-Pressing, page 24).

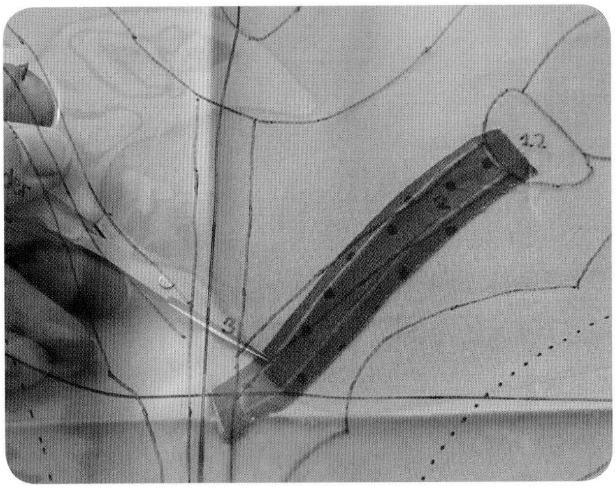

Use overlay to position hand appliqué pieces.

7. For hand appliqué, fold back the overlay and pin the appliqué pieces in place using 5/8″ Essential Appliqué Pins (see Resources, page 79). We usually position and stitch only a piece or 2 at a time. Remove the vinyl overlay before stitching.

Finger-Pressing

This is a very important step in needle-turn hand appliqué—whether you are sewing with an invisible stitch or making stitches with attitude. As you finger-press, make sure that the drawn line is pressed to the back. You'll be amazed at how much easier this one step makes needle-turning the turn-under allowance.

To finger-press, hold the appliqué piece right side up. Using your thumb and index finger, turn the turn-under allowance to the back of the appliqué so that the drawn line is just barely turned under.

Use your fingers to press a crease into the fabric along the inside of the drawn line. Good quality 100% cotton and linen will hold a finger-press very well. Do not wet your fingers, use starch, or scrape your fingernail along the crease. Just pinch it with your fingertips. Finger-press every edge that will be hand sewn down.

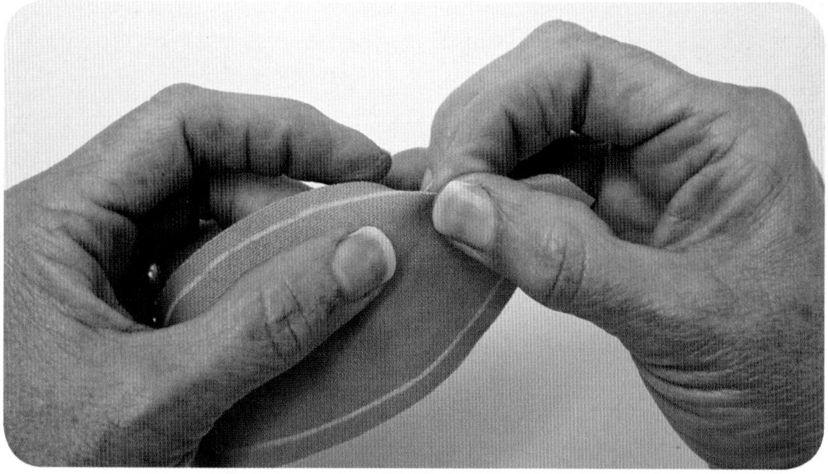

Finger-press turn-under allowance on each piece.

Pressing and Trimming the Blocks

1. After the appliqué is complete, press the blocks on the wrong side. Be careful not to stretch the blocks as you press. Use a pressing cloth with felted wool because wool scorches easily.
2. Take your time when trimming the blocks to size. Be sure of the measurements *before* you cut. Remember to measure twice and cut once.
3. Place a pressed block on the rotary cutting mat, right side up.
4. When you are sure you have measured correctly, trim the excess fabric from each side of the block.

Trimming Tips

- Always look carefully at the block before you trim. If you follow the cutting instructions in this book, you should be trimming off about ³⁄₄˝ from each edge of the blocks. If you are about to trim much more (or less) than that, check the measurements.
- Use the short lines that you drew over the ends of the pressed-in grid to help you center the cuts.
- Take your time. If it helps you visualize how much you need to trim away, compare the paper pattern with the block.

Stitches for Appliquéing with Felted Wool

Choosing Thread

Before you begin stitching, you need to select thread. Aurifil's wool thread is a 50% acrylic/50% wool blend, and it is our first choice when appliquéing felted wool. When we don't have the right color of wool thread, our next favorite thread is Presencia Finca Perlé Cotton thread in size 16 or 12.

If you want the stitches to be less visible, choose thread that is a close match to the appliqué fabric in both color and value.

If you want the stitches to show, choose a thread that contrasts in color with the appliqué fabric, use thicker threads, or combine different kinds of threads such as embroidery floss, metallic thread, sock yarn, thin silk ribbon, and more.

You can also add embellishments that suit your project, such as beads, buttons, sequins, and more. Use a thread that blends so as not to detract from the embellishments.

Embellishments are best added after quilting so that they are not in the way as you quilt. It is a good idea to sew heavy embellishments to the quilt through all of the layers.

Add embellishments that suit the project *after* quilting.

Refer to Felted Wool Preparation (page 14).

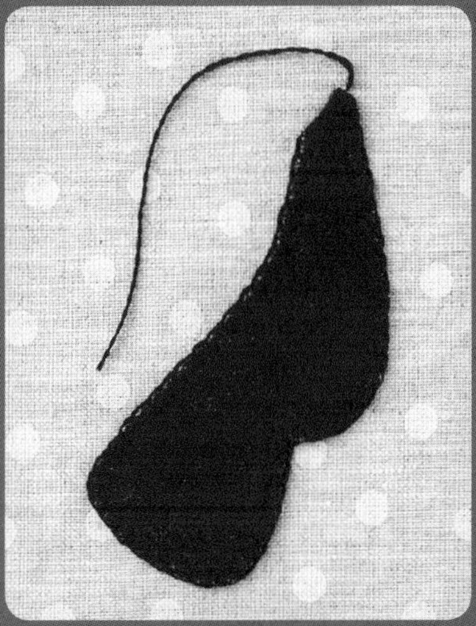

For less visible stitches, sew with thread that matches appliqué fabric.

For more visible stitches, sew with contrasting thread or threads.

The Blanket Stitch

We use a blanket stitch to stitch felted wool appliqué pieces in place. It holds the edges of the felted wool securely in place. Practice this stitch to see how far you want to bring the needle up, inside the edge. The bigger the stitch, the more visible it will be.

Choose the flattest spot to begin stitching on shapes that you sew all the way around. Do not begin sewing at either an inner or an outer point.

1. Bring the needle up from underneath the background fabric, at the edge of the appliqué, at 1.

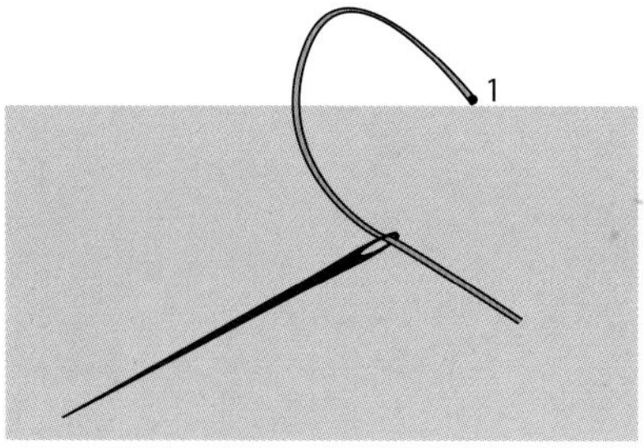

Bring needle up at 1.

2. Move to the left about ¼″ and down (away from the edge of the appliqué) about ¼″. Push the needle through the appliqué and the background at 2 so that it comes up through the background at the edge of the appliqué at 3. Hold the thread next to the block so that the tip of the needle comes up, over the thread.

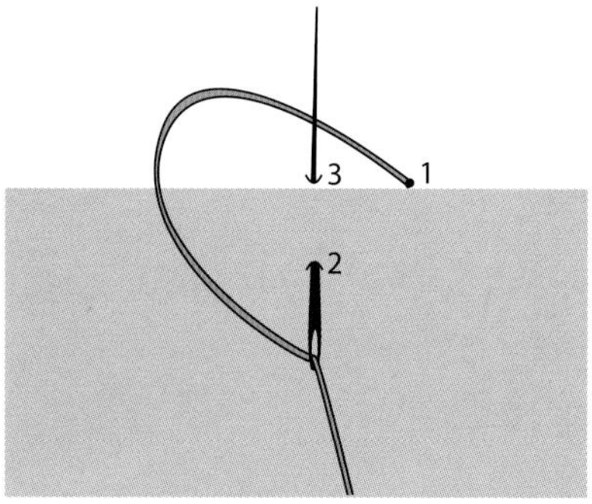

Push needle through at 2 and come back up, over thread, at 3.

3. Pull the stitches until they are snug against the edge of the appliqué, but do not pull them so tight that they cause the fabric to pucker. Continue sewing, making stitches that are the same size and are evenly spaced.

   Keep enough tension on the thread to pull the stitches into place against the edge of the appliqué. The stitches will look better if you pull the thread away from the edge of the appliqué.

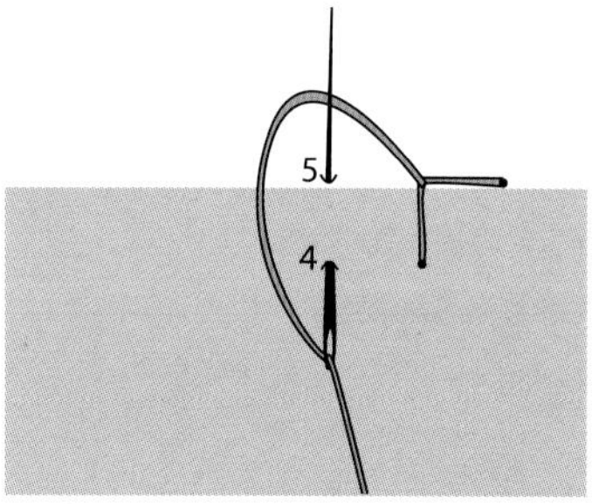

Continue sewing, making stitches that are evenly spaced.

4. To end a line of stitches, push the needle over the corner of the last loop, at the edge of the appliqué and take the needle to the back. Turn the block over and take 3 backstitches to secure the thread.

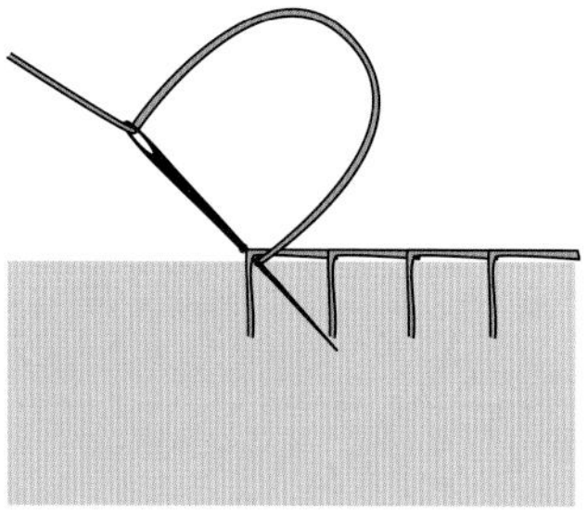

Stitch Length

Each blanket stitch is L-shaped. Each leg of the L should be the same length. In the instructions above, the stitch is ¼″. This length is appropriate in some spots—along the side of a large leaf, for example.

A smaller stitch is called for as shapes become smaller, pointed, round, or more intricate.

When One Piece Is Over Another

Due to the thickness of felted wool, when you are sewing one appliqué piece on top of another, it is important that each stitch go all the way through to the block background. You may need to pull the needle and thread to the back of the block in areas that have lots of stacked pieces.

Embellish with a Stem Stitch

The stem stitch is a good choice when you want to embroider lines, such as leaf veins.

1. Bring the needle up from underneath the background fabric, at the beginning of the line of stitches, at 1.

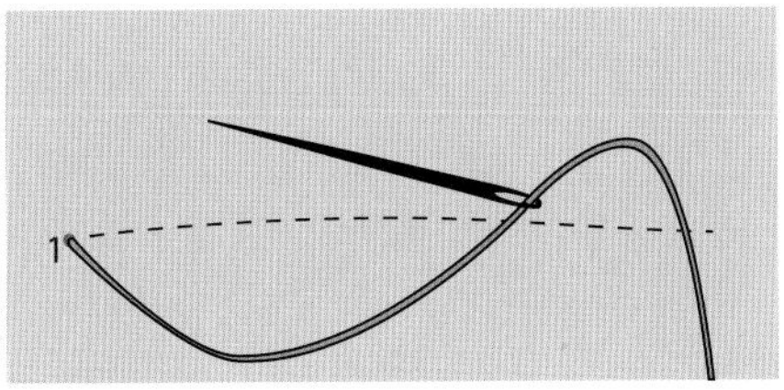

Bring needle up at 1.

2. Move to the right about ¼″ and push the needle through the fabric at 2. Do not pull the needle to the back of the block. Instead, turn the needle so that it comes up midway between 1 and 2, at 3. Hold the thread below the line, making sure the needle is above the stitch.

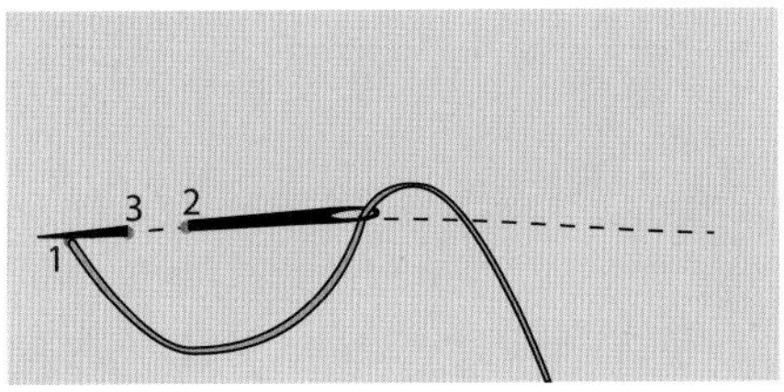

Push needle through at 2 and come back up at 3 (between 1 and 2).

3. Pull the needle and thread through the fabric to tighten the stitch so that it lies flat but does not cause the fabric to pucker.

4. Move to the right about ¼″ from 3 (which is ⅛″ from 2) and push the needle through the fabric at 4. Turn the needle and come up at 2 in the hole in the fabric formed by the last stitch.

Be sure to hold the thread so that it drapes over the previous stitch as you make each new stitch.

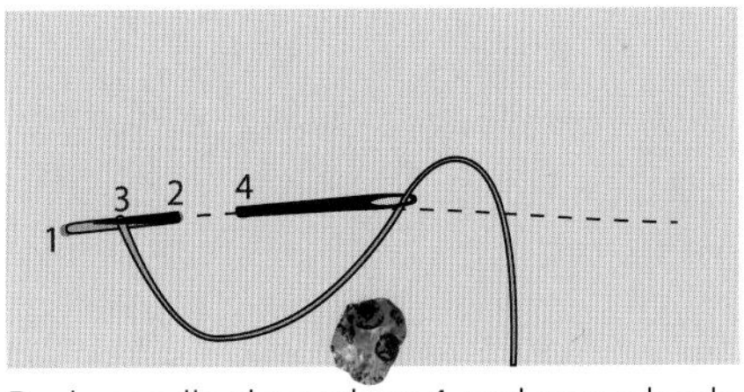

Push needle through at 4 and come back up at 2, at end of previous stitch.

5. Continue in this manner, keeping the stitches uniform in length and tension.

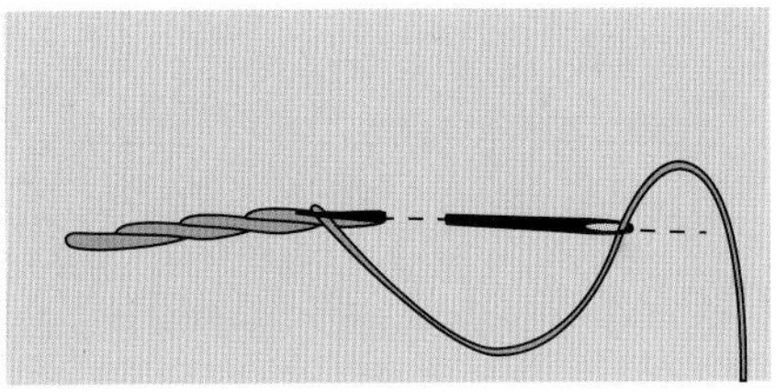

Keep stitches uniform in length and tension.

Look at the Back

If you turn over the block, the stitches should form a line from end to end.

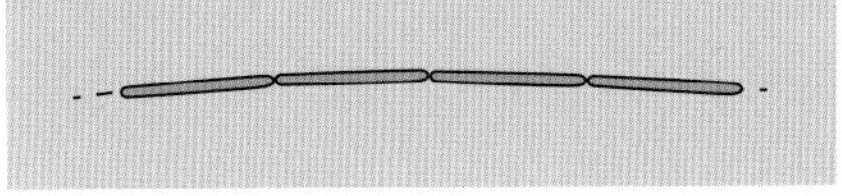

Stitches on back should be in line from end to end.

Special Techniques for Appliquéing with Felted Wool

Outer Points

You need to take special care when appliquéing points in felted wool because felted wool is thick and soft. By adjusting the stitch you can keep the points sharp and the stitches pretty.

1. When you are 2 or 3 stitches away from an outer point, begin making shorter stitches.

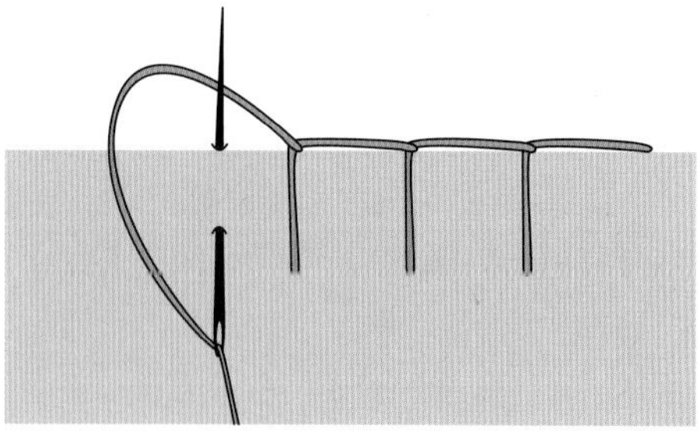

Begin making shorter stitches.

2. These shorter stitches are smaller than your regular stitch, so it will take more of them to reach the point. You may need more, or fewer, than are shown in the illustration. The points will look better if the stitches get smaller incrementally.

   Keep enough tension on the thread to pull the stitches into place against the edge of the appliqué. The stitches will look better if you pull the thread away from the edge of the appliqué.

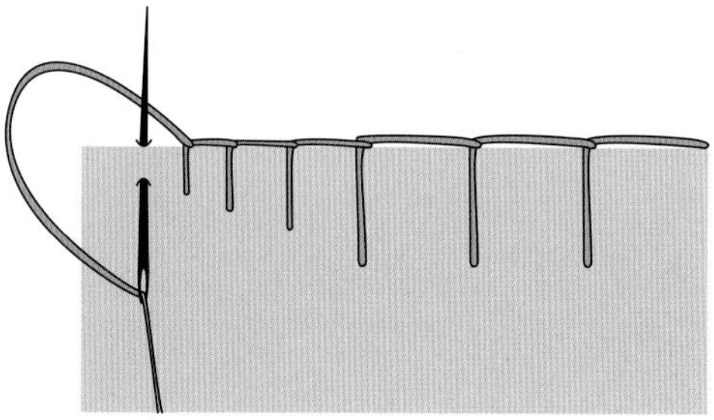

Make stitches incrementally shorter.

Tulip showing inner and outer points

Refer to Felted Wool Preparation (page 14).

3. When you make the stitch at the point, bring the needle out of the background fabric a little farther away from the edge than you normally would. This will help to keep this stitch from rolling underneath the edge of the appliqué and making the point look soft.

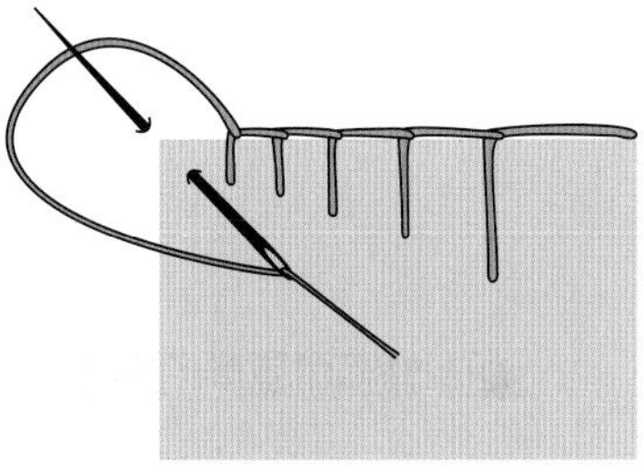

Corner stitch comes out beyond appliqué.

4. As you turn the corner, do your best to mirror the stitch length from the first side of the point.

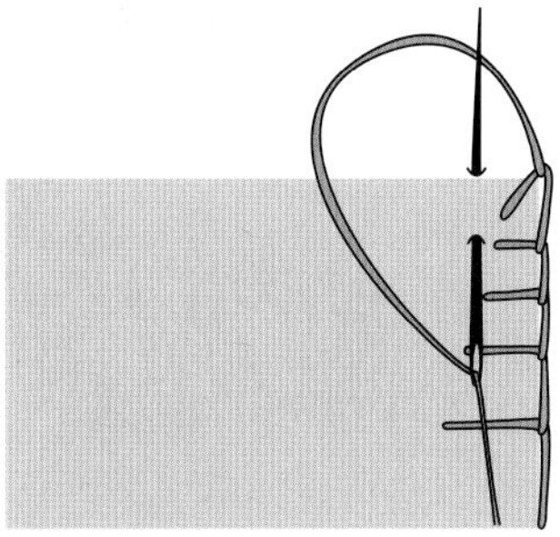

Mirror stitches after you turn corner.

5. You can go back to your normal stitch length when you are past the point.

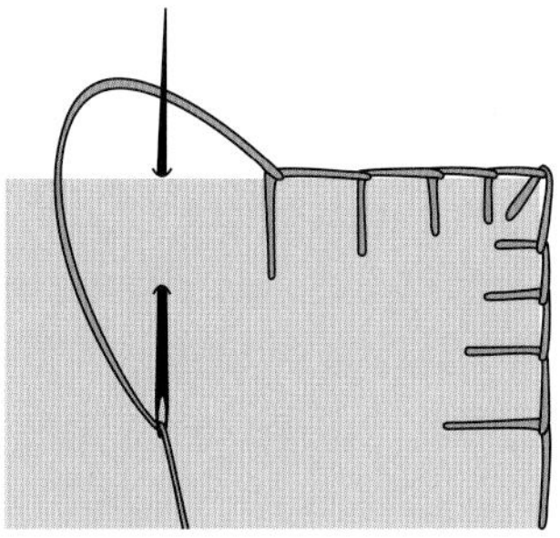

Resume regular stitch length.

Inner Points

Inner points are handled in much the same way outer points are, with stitches getting smaller then bigger on either side of the point. These shorter stitches are smaller than your regular stitch so it will take more of them to reach the point. You may need more, or fewer, than are shown in the illustration. The points will look better if the stitches get smaller incrementally.

Keep enough tension on the thread to pull the stitches into place against the edge of the appliqué. Your stitches will look better if you pull the thread away from the edge of the appliqué.

1. When you are 2 or 3 stitches away from an inner point, begin making shorter stitches. The last stitch on the first side of the inner point will be in line with the edge of the appliqué on the other side of the point.

   When you make this stitch, bring the needle out of the background fabric next to the edge of the appliqué, at the deepest part of the inner point.

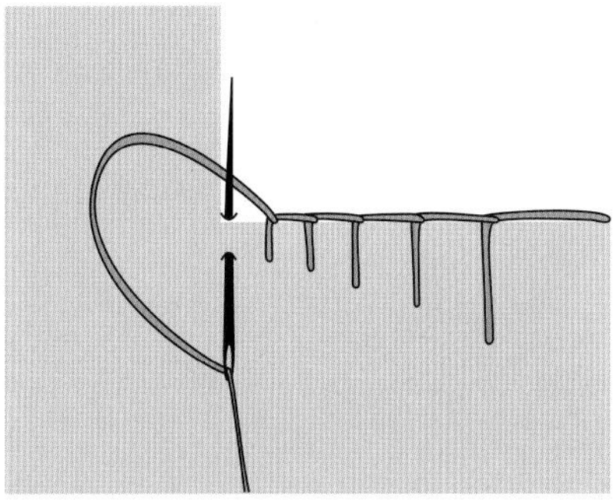

Bring out needle at edge of appliqué.

2. The stitch at the inner point is made on the diagonal and is spaced evenly between the 2 sides of the point. As you make this stitch, bring the point of the needle up through the same hole made by the previous stitch.

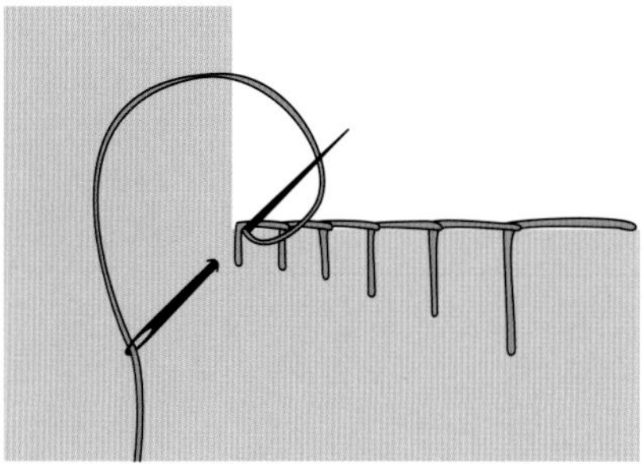

Diagonal stitch comes up through hole made by previous stitch.

3. As you turn the corner, do your best to mirror the stitch length from the first side of the point. Again, bring the point of the needle up through the same hole made by the previous 2 stitches.

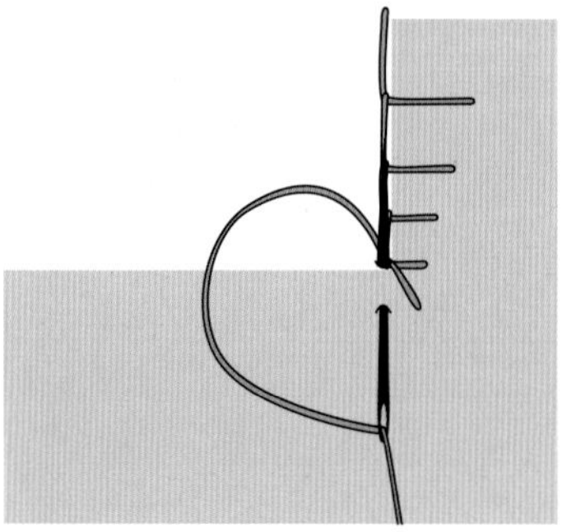

Mirror stitches after you turn corner.

4. The stitches at the inner point should resemble a chicken foot.

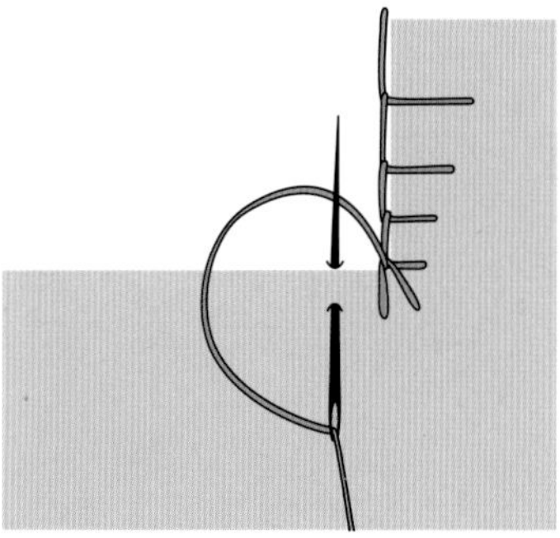

Three inner stitches come up through same hole.

5. You can go back to your normal stitch length once you are past the point.

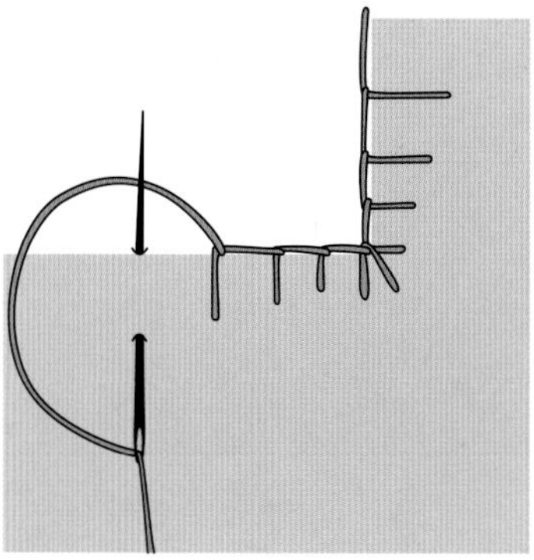

Resume regular stitch length.

Curves and Circles

The length of the stitches on curved appliqué shapes is determined by the acuteness of the curve and whether you are sewing an inner or an outer curve. The tighter the curve, the smaller the stitches need to be. This is true on any curved edge, including circles.

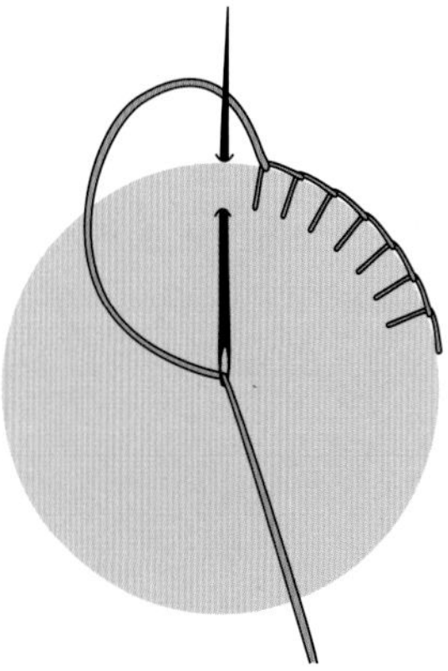

Tighter curves require smaller stitches.

How can you tell it's time to shorten the stitch? Keep an eye on the way the appliqué looks as you are sewing. If your stitch is too big it tends to roll under the edge of the appliqué as you sew, making the edge look less round than it is.

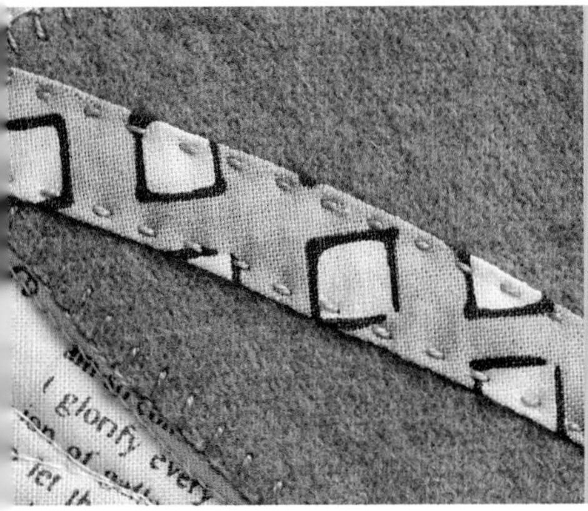

Appliqué with Attitude on Cotton

An appliqué stitch with attitude is one that is both very visible and decorative in its own right. The running stitch is a good choice to use in these projects.

Detail of running stitch from *Jamestown Avenue* (page 67)

We use Presencia Finca Perlé Cotton thread in either size 12 or size 16. Size 12 is a little thicker and therefore more visible. Size 16 is thinner and pulls through the fabric a little more easily.

Sharp needles in size 7 or 9 work with both of these weights of perle cotton, as does Bohin's size 9 crewel needle. If you need a needle threader, try using the hand-held Quilter's Needle Threader by Collins.

The Running Stitch

This stitch will feel familiar to those of you who have hand quilted. The stitches create a dashed line that accentuates the edge of the appliqué.

1. Prepare an appliqué piece as you would for regular needle-turn appliqué (see Using the Templates to Appliqué with Attitude, page 21). Finger-press the shape (see Finger-Pressing, page 24) and pin it to the block.
2. Bring up the needle through the appliqué fabric about 1⁄16″ inside the finger-pressed crease that is at the inside edge of the drawn line. Use the needle to turn under the turn-under allowance and hold it in place with the finger and thumb of your holding hand. The knot and the thread tail will be buried under the appliqué.

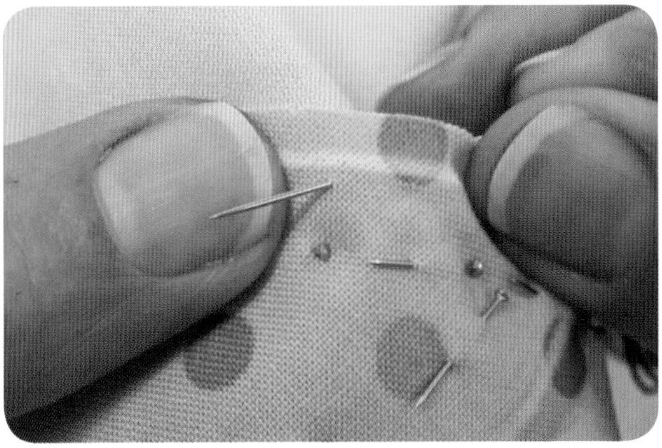

Bring up needle inside finger-pressed crease.

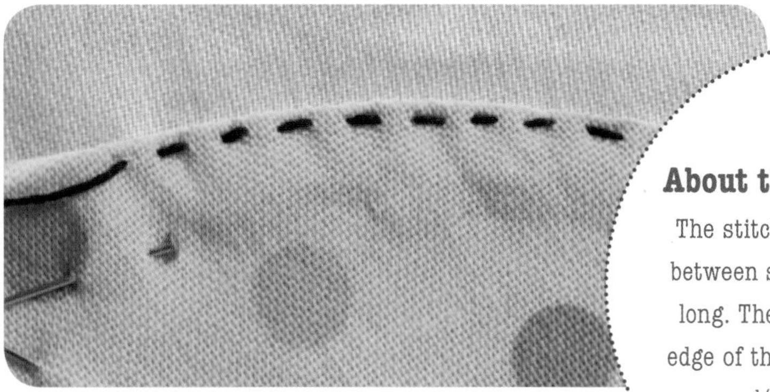
Stitch length and space between should be equal.

About the Running Stitch

The stitch length and the space between stitches will be ¹⁄₁₆″–⅛″ long. The needle will follow the edge of the appliqué and be about ¹⁄₁₆″ away from it.

3. Stitch from right to left (if you are right-handed). Hold the block so that the edge of the appliqué is running from side to side. Your left thumb should be sitting directly on top of the folded edge and be positioned so that when you stitch, the needle is pointed at the end of your thumb, not the side of your thumb.
4. Place the needle a stitch length to the left of the point where you brought up the thread. Push the needle straight down through the appliqué and the background until you hit the tip of your underneath finger.
5. Rock over your underneath finger and push the needle back up through the background and the folded edge of the appliqué. Try to make the stitches and spaces between them uniform. Really bend over the bottom finger so that the needle travels as straight as it can up through the layers. Keep pinching together the fabric using your left finger and thumb to keep the layers together and to help you make the stitch length you prefer.

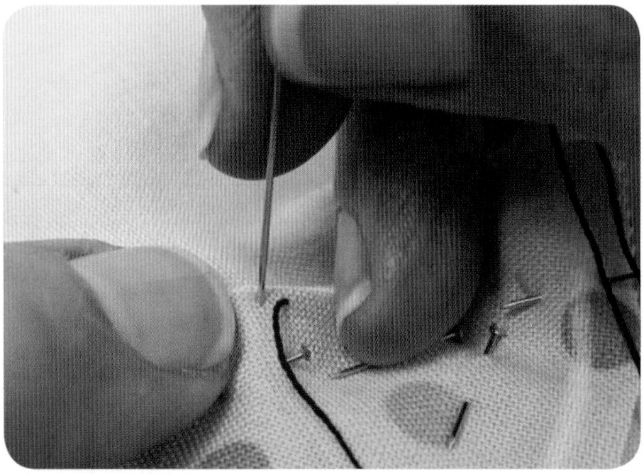
Push needle straight down through appliqué and background.

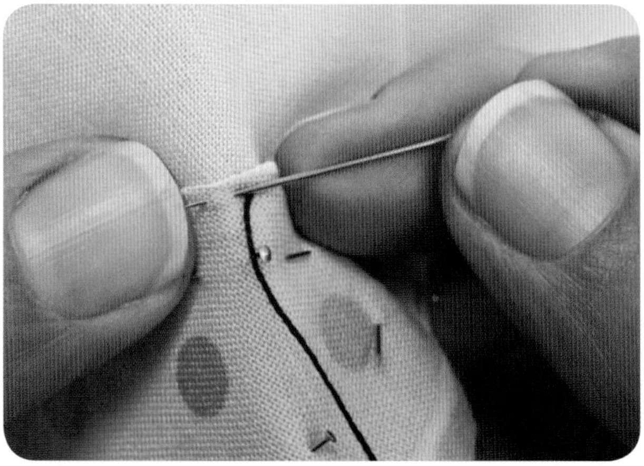
Rock needle back and forth to load stitches.

6. Unless the fabric is very tightly woven, you can pack 2–4 stitches on the needle at a time. Push the needle up only the length of a single stitch and then point it right back down through the layers until you can feel it with your bottom finger.

   Push the needle down until it feels like you have gone the distance you want to go, and then bend it back up over your bottom finger.

Load 2–4 stitches on needle.

7. When you think you have all the stitches you can make on the needle, pull the needle and thread through the fabric. Don't pull the thread so tight that you pleat the edges, but don't leave the thread loose either.

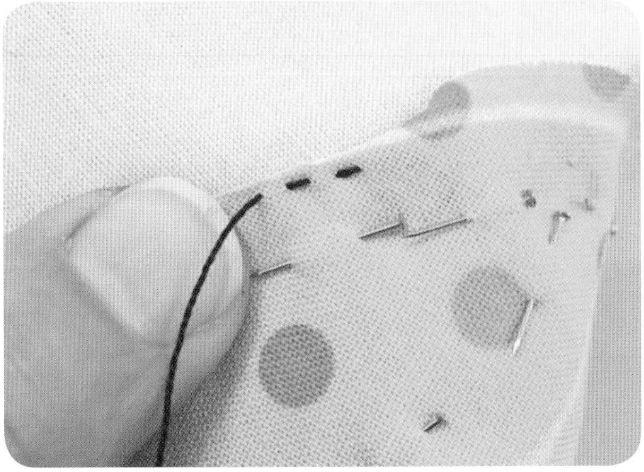

Pull thread snug.

8. Continue in this manner, turning under the edges along the finger-pressed crease, rocking the needle up and down to make the stitches.

Ending a Running Stitch

Because the first running stitch is brought up through the appliqué only, the beginning of that stitch is not held tightly to the background. There are some shapes that you stitch all the way around until you are back to the first stitch. In these cases, stitch over your first stitch with your last stitch, and then knot the fabric on the back, burying the tail of thread before cutting it. To end, knot your thread on the back. Run the needle between the background and appliqué fabrics about ½″, pull through the back and cut your thread, burying the tail.

Finishing Techniques

Finishing the Quilt

1. Construct the back of the quilt, piecing as needed.
2. Place the backing right side down on a firm surface. Tape it down with painter's tape to keep it from moving around while you baste, but don't stretch it.
3. Place the batting over the backing and *pat* out any wrinkles.
4. Center the quilt top right side up over the batting.
5. Thread-baste the layers together. Yes, we thread-baste for both hand and machine quilting.
6. Quilt by machine or by hand (see Quilting Felted Wool, page 35).
7. Trim the outer edges of the quilt, leaving ¼″ of backing and batting extending beyond the edge of the quilt top. This extra fabric and batting will fill the binding nicely.
8. Finish the outer edges with continuous bias binding (see Continuous Bias Binding, page 36).
9. Make a hanging sleeve and label, and attach them to the back of the quilt.

Trim outer edges of quilt, leaving ½″ of backing and batting beyond edge of quilt top.

Freshen It Up

Quilts with felted wool appliqué can be freshened up with a quick toss in a dryer set to air dry (no heat). This helps to remove dust and fluff them up.

Quilting Felted Wool

When quilting quilts made with cotton fabric, we usually quilt in-the-ditch around the edges of the appliqué. If you quilt in-the-ditch around felted wool appliqué shapes, the quilting tends to make the appliqué puff out too much.

Whether you are quilting by hand or machine, what works better is to quilt the background lightly, and not too close to the edges of the appliqué. Too much quilting will distort the appliqué. The same is true with quilting inside the appliqué shapes—less is better.

When you are trying to decide on a pattern to quilt in the background, look to the fabric first. If there is a pattern in the background fabric, you can quilt around the motifs. If that isn't an option, choose a pattern that complements the appliqué design and that is not too tight.

We recommend that you use a 40-weight cotton thread, such as King Tut by Superior Threads, for machine quilting felted wool projects. It is a nice weight to use with the thick felted wool fabrics, especially when you are quilting through multiple layers of felted wool.

Use a closed-toe foot, if you have one, when machine quilting a quilt with felted wool appliqué. The blanket stitches at the edges of the shapes can get hung up on an open-toe foot.

If you are hand quilting, you can use a hoop or not. If you use a hoop, put the quilt in the hoop but don't tighten the outer ring. Press down with your hand to loosen the tension on the quilt; then tighten the hoop.

Hand quilted stitches made with perle cotton thread look great with felted wool appliqué. This thicker thread holds its own next to the thick felted wool. When hand quilting with perle cotton, use any of the needles listed in Basic Supplies (page 7). Make stitches that are ⅛″ long, or longer.

You can combine hand quilting with perle cotton and machine quilting—or you can quilt the entire project by hand or by machine.

Quilting through Multiple Layers

It is next to impossible to hand quilt through two or more layers of felted wool. If you want to quilt in these areas, quilt by machine. If you do decide to hand quilt, take your needle to the back of the quilt with each stitch. This is called stick-and-stab quilting or stab-stitch quilting.

Some of the quilts in this book are both hand and machine quilted.

Continuous Bias Binding

Fabric strips cut on the bias are stretchy. These stretchy strips are perfect for binding, cording, bias stems, and piping. Make a *continuous bias strip* when you need more than a short length of bias. A surprisingly small amount of fabric makes quite a bit of bias with no waste.

We make continuous bias strips 2½″ wide for binding and 2″ wide for cording; the size of the square you begin with determines how long the continuous bias strip will be. Refer to the specific project instructions for the size of the square needed for that project.

1. Start with a square of fabric and cut it in half diagonally.

2. Sew together the 2 triangles, right sides together, as shown. Be sure to sew the edges that are on the straight of grain.

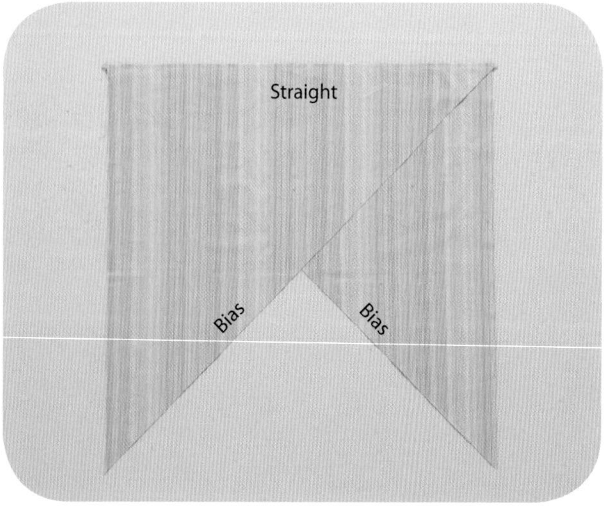

Sew together straight-of-grain edges of triangles.

3. Press the seam allowances open. Make a short cut 2½″ wide (2″ wide for cording) into each side as shown.

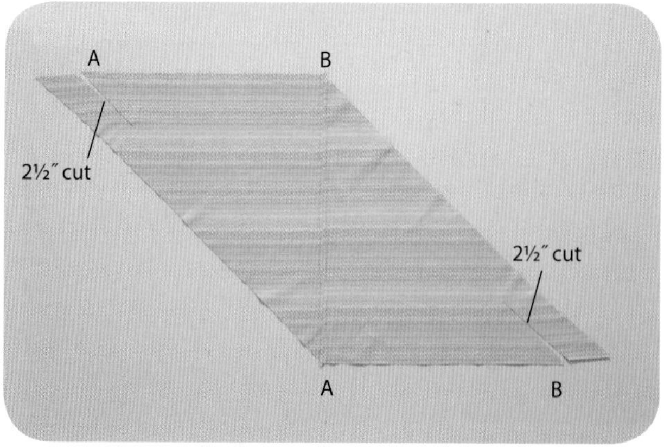

Make short cut into each side.

4. Match the A's and B's with the fabric right sides together. Pin and sew. Press the seam open.

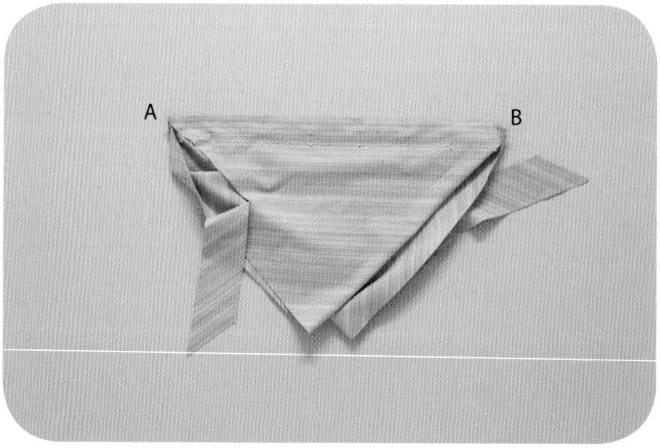

Pin and sew; press seam open.

5. You have sewn the fabric into a tube. Use a rotary cutter and ruler to cut the continuous bias strip 2½″ wide (2″ wide for cording) from a single side of the tube.

6. Press the binding strip in half lengthwise, wrong sides together. It is now ready to use to bind the edges of the quilt.

Straight-Grain Binding from Strips

1. Cut strips across the width of the fabric as designated by the pattern. Angle both ends at the same 45° angle.

2. Place 2 strips right sides together. Offset the ends so that a V is formed at the ¼″ seamline.

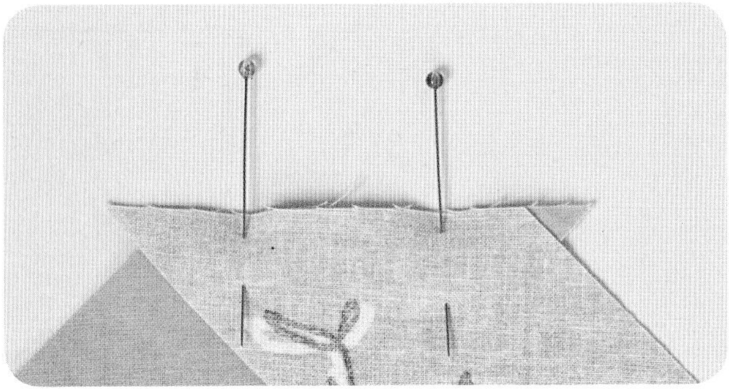

Offset ends and sew together strips.

3. Sew together the strips, end to end, with a ¼″ seam. Press the seams open. Trim away the dog-ears that extend beyond the edges of the strips.

4. Press the binding strip in half lengthwise, wrong sides together. Be sure to use a walking foot to sew this binding to the quilt.

Sewing Binding to the Quilt

It works best to sew binding to the quilt with a walking foot.

1. Make a continuous bias strip 2½″ wide by the length specified in the pattern. (Refer to Continuous Bias Binding, page 36).
2. Cut the first end of the strip at a 45° angle. Turn under this end ½″ and press.
3. Press the binding strip in half lengthwise, wrong sides together.
4. With raw edges even, pin the binding to the edge of the quilt top beginning a few inches away from a corner. Start sewing 6″ from the beginning of the binding strip, using a ¼″ seam allowance.
5. Stop ¼″ away from the corner and backstitch several stitches.
6. Fold the binding straight up as shown. Note the 45° angle.

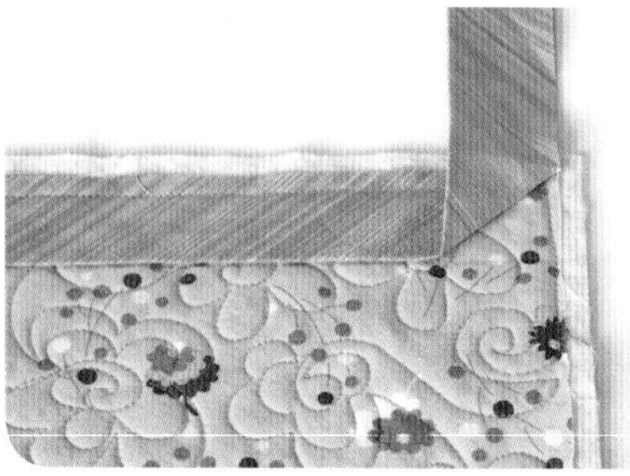

Fold binding up.

7. Fold the binding straight down, pin in place, and begin sewing the next side of the quilt.

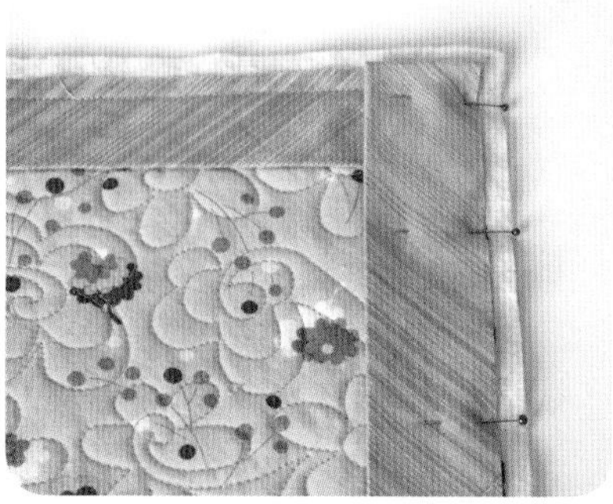

Fold binding down and begin sewing.

8. Sew the binding to all sides of the quilt, following the process in Steps 5–7. Stop a few inches before you reach the beginning of the binding, but don't trim the excess binding yet.
9. Overlap the ends of the binding and cut the second end square. Be sure to cut the binding long enough so that the cut end is covered completely by the angled end.
10. Slip the squared end into the angled end.

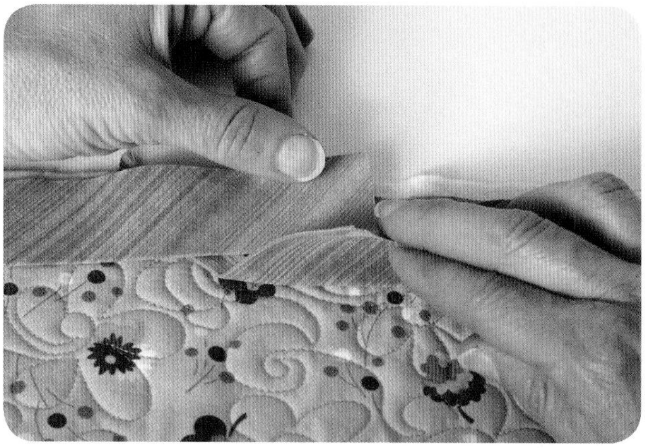

Slip squared end into angled end.

11. Pin the joined ends to the quilt and finish sewing the binding to the quilt.

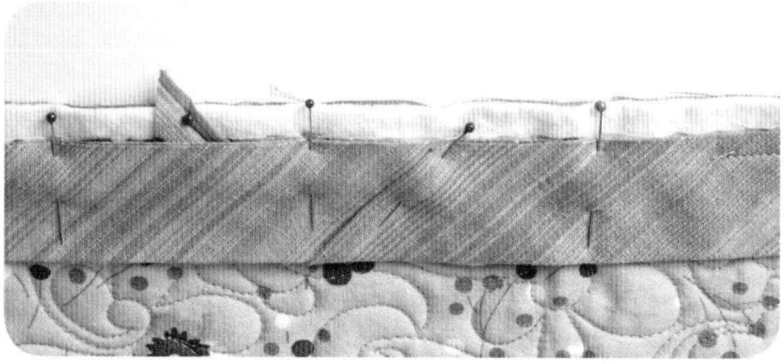

Pin and finish sewing.

12. Turn the binding to the back of the quilt, covering the raw edges. If there is too much batting, trim some to leave the binding nicely filled. Hand stitch the folded edge of the binding to the back of the quilt.

Piping

Piping makes a very nice edge on any pillow, including the leaf pillows in this book (Leafy Pillows, page 62).

1. Make a strip of continuous bias binding (see Continuous Bias Binding, page 36). Cut the strip 2″ wide for cording.
2. *Gently* press the continuous bias strip in half lengthwise, wrong sides together.
3. Cut the first end of the bias strip at a 90° angle. Turn this end under 1″, and press.
4. Place ¼″ cotton piping cord down the lengthwise fold of the bias strip, ½″ from the first end of the strip.

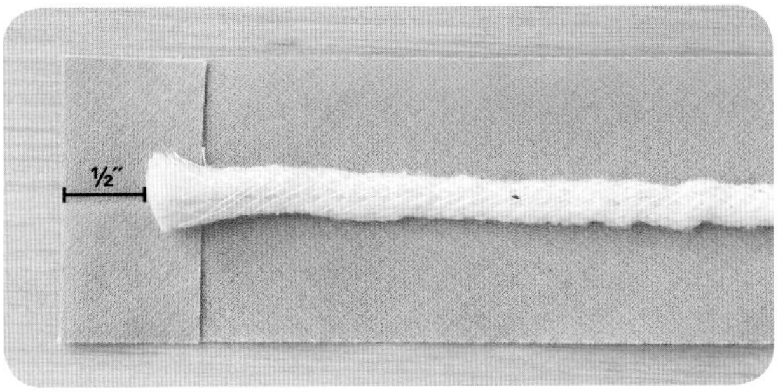

Place piping cord ½″ from first end of strip.

5. Using a zipper foot and matching thread, sew the piping cord into the bias strip beginning ¾″ from the beginning of the strip. Use a relatively long stitch length.
6. Trim excess fabric, leaving a ¼″ seam allowance. *Do not trim excess fabric at the first end of the strip*—you'll want this fabric to hold onto when you hide the end of the cord.

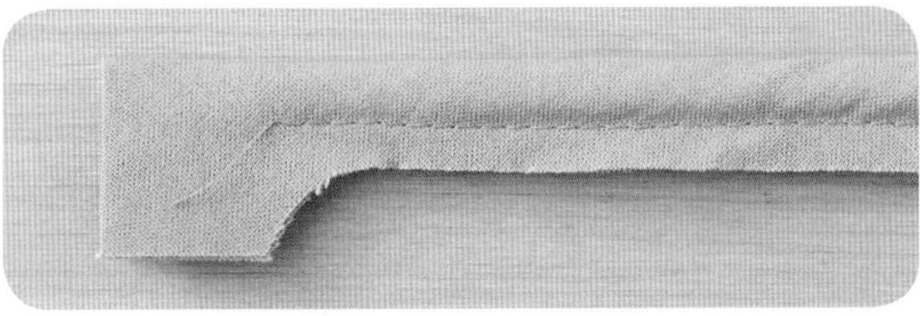

Trim excess fabric next to cotton cord, leaving ¼″ seam allowance. *Do not trim excess fabric at first end of strip.*

7. With raw edges even, pin the cording to the edge of the pillow front. Do not begin at a corner.
8. Start sewing ¾″ away from the beginning of the cording strip, using a ¼″ seam allowance, matching thread, a long stitch length, and the zipper foot. The corners will be rounded. Make sure that they all have the same degree of roundness.

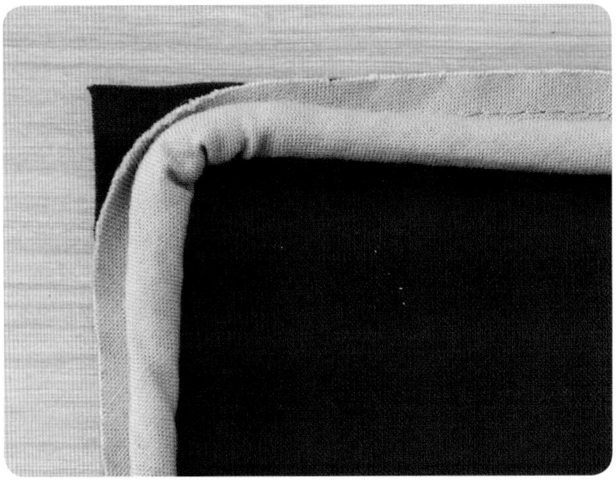

Corners will be rounded; make sure they all have same degree of roundness.

9. Work your way around the pillow top. When you get back to the beginning, cut the cording so that it is even with the end of the cotton cord that lies inside the first end. Nestle the cut end inside the first end of the cording. Sew it in place. Cut off the excess fabric at the beginning of the strip.

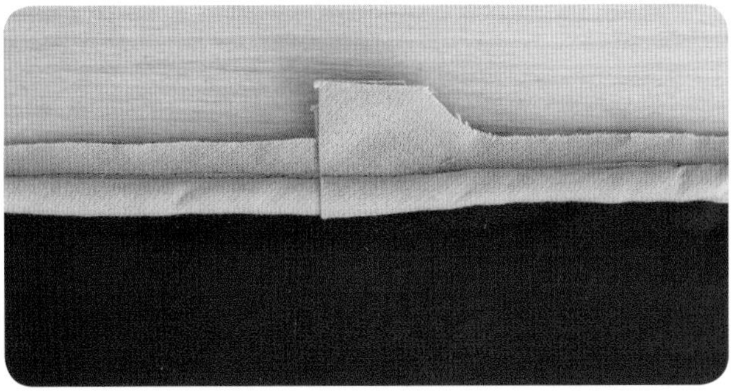

Nestle ends of cording together and sew cording in place.

Projects

Blue Basket

FINISHED QUILT SIZE: 22″ × 34″

Made by Linda Jenkins

A lovely riot of flowers is anchored by a cute little basket in this charming small quilt. It is perfect to use on the wall or table.

Materials

Fabric note: Linda used the same vintage fabric for her block background and binding.

- Block background fabric: ⅝ yard
- Inner border: ¼ yard
- Outer border: ¼ yard
- Appliqué fabrics: A variety of large scraps of felted wool
- Binding: ⅔ yard
- Backing and sleeve: 1¼ yards
- Batting: 30″ × 42″

Additional supplies

- Self-adhesive laminating sheets: 6 sheets
- Clear vinyl: ½ yard of 54″ wide *OR* ¾ yard of 16″–18″ wide
- Fusible web: 6 sheets of SoftFuse *OR* ⅔ yard of 18″-wide fusible
- Appliqué threads: Aurifil wool in colors to match or complement the fabrics
- Aqua ½″ rickrack: 3½ yards
- Aqua ¼″ rickrack: ½ yard, for basket trim

Cutting

WOF = width of fabric

Block background fabric

Cut 1 rectangle 18″ × 30″.

Inner border

Cut 3 strips 1½″ × WOF.

Subcut 2 strips 1½″ × 16½″ for the side borders.

Subcut 2 strips 1½″ × 30½″ for the top and bottom borders.

Outer border

Cut 3 strips 2½″ × WOF.

Subcut 2 strips 2½″ × 18½″ for the side borders.

Subcut 2 strips 2½″ × 34½″ for the top and bottom borders.

Binding

Cut 1 square 22″ × 22″ to make a 2½″-wide continuous bias strip 130″ long for the binding (see Continuous Bias Binding, page 36).

Block Assembly

Refer to General Appliqué Instructions (page 17) as needed.

Appliqué placement

1. Make templates and overlays for the block using the *Blue Basket* patterns (pullout page P2).
2. Press the background in half horizontally and vertically. Place it on your design wall.
3. Refer to Preparing to Stitch (page 14) to choose fabrics, fuse the fusible web to all the felted wool appliqués, and cut them out.
4. Place the appliqué pieces on the background on your design wall. Use the overlay to place the appliqué pieces in the proper position, or place them by eye. Play with color and fabric choices until you are happy with the way the block looks.
5. Hand sew the ¼″ rickrack to the vase before fusing it to the block. Turn the ends of the rickrack to the back of the vase and secure them with a few stitches or, if that seems too bulky, trim the ends even with the edges of the vase and carefully stitch them down.
6. Fuse and appliqué the block; Linda used the blanket stitch. Select your appliqué stitch from Stitches for Appliquéing with Felted Wool (page 25).
7. When the appliqué is complete, press the block on the wrong side, and trim it to 16½″ × 28½″.

Quilt Assembly

Refer to quilt assembly diagram (below) for quilt construction. Seam allowances are ¼″.

1. Place the block, inner border strips, and outer border strips on the design wall.
2. Sew the left and right inner border strips to the block. Press the seam allowances toward the inner border.
3. Sew an inner border strip to the top and bottom of the block. Press the seam allowances toward the inner border.
4. Sew the left and right outer border strips to the sides of the quilt. Press the seam allowances toward the outer border.
5. Sew the top and bottom outer border strips to the top and bottom of the quilt. Press the seam allowances toward the outer border.
6. Layer and baste the quilt. Quilt by hand or machine—or both—and bind. Linda hand quilted the background and inside some of the yellow flowers. She machine quilted the yellow inner border (refer to Finishing Techniques, page 34).
7. Pin the ½″ rickrack to the border. Use a free-motion foot and machine quilt the rickrack to the quilt, through all layers. When you work your way around the quilt and back to the beginning of the rickrack, turn the raw edge under. Match the curves in the rickrack and sew the end in place, hiding the raw end.

   If the rickrack edges curl, you can sew them down by hand.

Quilt assembly

Yo-Yo Garden Foot Warmer

FINISHED QUILT SIZE: 18″ × 50″

Made by Linda Jenkins and Mildred Phillips

Linda took stems of flowers out of *Blue Basket* (page 44) and planted them in this quilt to be placed at the foot of her bed. Look closely and you'll find the flowers made from yo-yos.

Materials

- Light tone-on-tone cotton background fabrics: A variety to total approximately 1 yard
- Appliqué fabrics: A variety of large scraps of felted wool for the stems, leaves, and flowers
- Cotton prints: 51 scraps 4″ × 4″ square to make yo-yos
- Red cotton border and binding fabric: 1 yard
- Backing and sleeve: 1¾ yards
- Batting: 26″ × 58″

Additional supplies

- Self-adhesive laminating sheets: 9 sheets
- Fusible web: 9 sheets of SoftFuse *OR* 1 yard of 18″-wide fusible
- Clear vinyl: ½ yard of 54″ wide *OR* 1½ yards of 16″–18″ wide
- Appliqué threads: Aurifil wool in colors to match or complement the fabrics
- Sewing thread: 2-ply or 3-ply regular cotton thread to tack the yo-yos to the block
- Quick Yo-Yo Maker (Small) from Clover (*optional*): This tool is very helpful in making 1¼″ (30 mm) yo-yos.

Alternate Option

If you prefer to use only one background fabric, cut or piece a rectangle 17″ × 52″.

Cutting

WOF = width of fabric

Light tone-on-tone block background fabrics

A's: Cut 8 squares 5½″ × 5½″.

B's: Cut 18 rectangles 5½″ × 6½″.

C's: Cut 4 squares 6½″ × 6½″.

Red border fabric

Cut 2 strips 1½″ × WOF for the top border.

Cut 2 strips 2½″ × WOF for the bottom border.

Binding

Cut 1 square 23″ × 23″ to make a 2½″-wide continuous bias strip 150″ long for the binding (see Continuous Bias Binding, page 36).

Quilt Assembly

Refer to General Appliqué Instructions (page 17) as needed. Seam allowances are ¼″.

1. Make templates for the quilt using the *Blue Basket* patterns (pullout page P2).

   Notes: The shape numbers in the appliqué placement diagram (below) are the same as those in *Blue Basket*. The stem labeled 3R indicates that template 3 has been turned upside down to create a mirror image (or reverse image) of the shape.

2. Draw a 15″ × 50″ rectangle on a long piece of paper or several smaller sheets of paper taped together to make a large sheet. Draw horizontal and vertical centerlines on the rectangle. Refer to the appliqué placement diagram (below) and place the templates on the paper. Use a 1¼″ circle to represent the yo-yos. They nest and, in some cases, overlap to form flowers.

3. Trace around the templates to make a pattern.

4. Make an overlay for the quilt from the pattern.

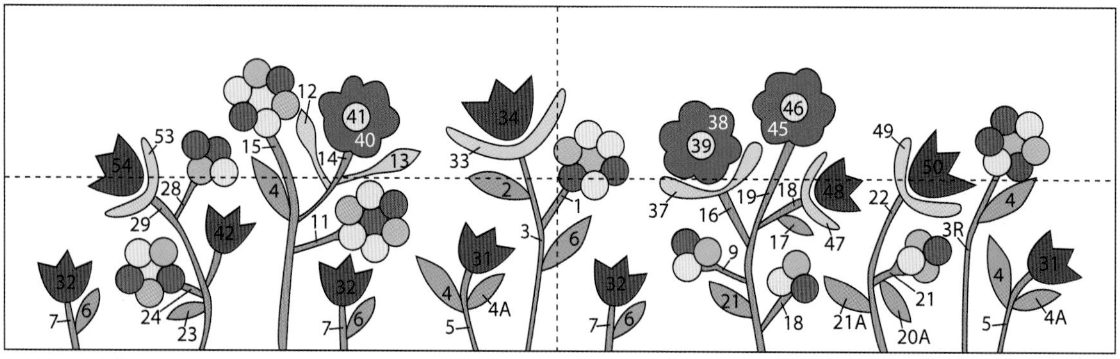

Appliqué placement

5. Place the A, B, and C background fabrics on your design wall. Play with their placement until you are happy with the way the background looks.

C	B	B	B	B	B	B	B	B	C
B	A	A	A	A	A	A	A	A	B
C	B	B	B	B	B	B	B	B	C

Background piecing

6. Sew together the background pieces into 3 horizontal rows. Press the seam allowances in the top and bottom rows to the right. Press the seam allowances in the center row to the left. Sew together the rows.

7. Press the background in half horizontally. (The vertical center will be marked by a sewn seamline.) Place the background on your design wall.

8. If you have the yo-yo maker from Clover, follow the instructions on the package and make 51 yo-yos. If you do not have a yo-yo maker, refer to Making Yo-Yos (page 74). Use the 3″ circle template from that chapter.

9. Refer to Preparing to Stitch (page 14) to choose fabrics, fuse the fusible web to all the felted wool appliqués, and cut them out.

10. Place the appliqué pieces and yo-yos on the background on your design wall. Use the overlay to place the appliqué pieces in the proper position, or place them by eye. Play with color and fabric choices until you are happy with the way the block looks.

11. Fuse and appliqué the felted wool shapes onto the block. Select your appliqué stitch from Stitches for Appliquéing with Felted Wool (page 25).

12. Stitch the yo-yos to the quilt top. The yo-yos will appear to be plumper if you stitch them more loosely to the block. However, if you think the quilt will be subjected to wear and tear, stitch them more securely to the block.

13. When the appliqué is complete, press the quilt top on the wrong side. Place the quilt top on a soft towel to prevent smashing the yo-yos. Trim the quilt top to 15½″ × 50½″.

14. Trim away the selvages at the ends of all the border strips. Sew together the top border strips end to end. Do the same for the bottom border strips.

15. Measure the quilt horizontally through the center and trim the border strips to fit.

16. Sew the top and bottom borders to the quilt. Press seam allowances toward the borders.

17. Layer and baste the quilt. Quilt by hand or machine, and bind. Refer to Finishing Techniques (page 34).

Quilt assembly

Fruitful Market Basket

FINISHED QUILT SIZE: 29″ × 24″

Made by Linda Jenkins

A delicious assortment of fruit is lovely in this pretty, woven market basket. Use this small quilt as a table topper or hang it on the wall.

Materials

Linda used a green cotton/linen blend for the background. The tablecloth is Kirman by Kaffe Fassett for Rowan.

- Cotton or linen block background fabric: ¾ yard
- Cotton or linen tablecloth fabric: ¼ yard
- Appliqué fabrics:

  Brown felted wool fabric for the basket body and handle: ½ yard

  Teal basket strips: 1 felted wool Chubby *OR* a piece 6″ × 18″

  Aqua basket strips: 1 felted wool Chubby *OR* a piece 6″ × 18″

  A variety of scraps of felted wool for the fruit
- Binding: ⅔ yard
- Backing and sleeve: 1⅓ yards
- Batting: 32″ × 37″

Additional supplies

- Self-adhesive laminating sheets: 18 sheets
- Fusible web: 17 sheets of SoftFuse *OR* 2 yards of 18″-wide fusible
- Clear vinyl: ¾ yard of 54″ wide *OR* 1½ yards of 16″–18″ wide (Tape vinyl together as necessary.)
- Appliqué threads: Aurifil wool in colors to match or complement the fabrics

Cutting

WOF = width of fabric

Block background fabric

Cut 1 rectangle 20¼″ × 31″.

Tablecloth fabric

Cut 1 rectangle 6¼″ × 31″.

Binding

Cut 1 square 21″ × 21″ to make a 2½″-wide continuous bias strip 130″ long for the binding (see Continuous Bias Binding, page 36).

Quilt Assembly

Refer to General Appliqué Instructions (page 17) as needed. Seam allowances are ¼″.

1. Make templates and overlays for the block using the *Fruitful Market Basket* patterns (pullout page P1).
2. Sew the tablecloth strip to the bottom of the background fabric. Press the seam allowances toward the tablecloth.
3. Press the background/tablecloth unit in half horizontally and vertically. Place it on your design wall.
4. Refer to Preparing to Stitch (page 14) to choose fabrics, fuse the fusible web to all the felted wool appliqués, and cut them out.
5. Place the appliqué pieces on the background on your design wall. Use the overlay to place the appliqué pieces in the proper position, or place them by eye. Play with color and fabric choices until you are happy with the way the block looks.

Appliqué placement

6. Fuse the pieces to the block. Be sure to weave the basket strips before fusing. Appliqué the block. Select your appliqué stitch from Stitches for Appliquéing with Felted Wool (page 25).

Sew a Bunch of Grapes

Note that on the *Fruitful Market Basket* patterns, there is an oval shape you can place under the grapes to make them look fuller.

Baste this oval piece into place, ⅛″ inside of the edge of the fabric, with matching thread.

It is also a good idea to sew all the way around each grape, even where a shape is covered by another shape. This adds dimension to the grapes.

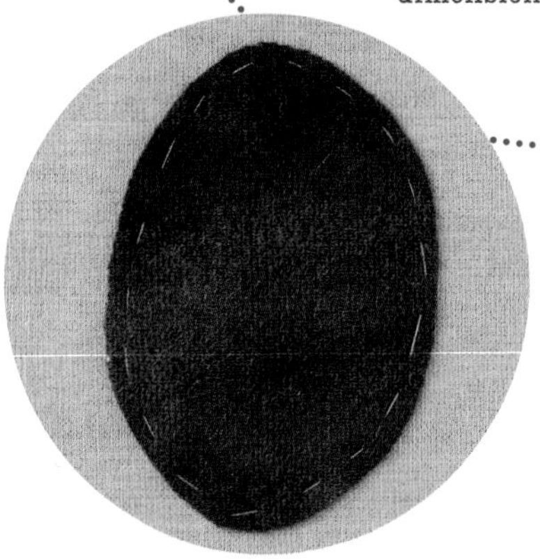

Baste grape base fabric in place.

7. When the appliqué is complete, press the block on the wrong side, and trim it to 29½″ × 24½″.
8. Layer and baste the quilt. Quilt by hand or machine, and bind. Refer to Finishing Techniques (page 34).

Strawberry Zip Bag

FINISHED SIZE: 9½″ × 8″

Made by Becky Goldsmith

Back of pouch

This handy pouch is both cute and functional. After you see how fast and easy it is to make, you'll want to make them for all your friends.

Materials

- Pouch front and zipper facing fabric: 1 fat quarter
- Lining fabric: 1 fat quarter
- Appliqué fabrics: A variety of scraps of felted wool
- Binding: 1 fat quarter

Additional supplies

- Self-adhesive laminating sheets: 1 sheet
- Clear vinyl for overlay and to sew into pouch: ¼ yard of 54″ wide *OR* ⅓ yard of 16″–18″ wide
- Fusible web:

  1 sheet of SoftFuse *OR* ⅛ yard of 18″-wide fusible for the appliqué

  AND

  1 piece 8½″ × 10″ or ¼ yard of 18″-wide fusible for the lining
- Appliqué threads: Perle cotton size 12 *OR* Aurifil wool in colors to match or complement the fabrics
- Nylon zipper, 16″ or longer: 1
- 1″ bias tape maker (*optional*)
- Wonder Clips or binding clips (*optional*)

Cutting

WOF = width of fabric

Pouch front and zipper facing fabric

Cut 1 rectangle 9½″ × 11″ for the pouch front.

Cut 2 strips 1½″ × 11″ for the zipper facing.

Lining fabric

Cut 1 rectangle 8½″ × 10″.

Clear vinyl

Cut 1 rectangle 5¾″ × 9½″.

Binding

Cut 2 strips 1¾″ wide × 24″ from the true bias of the fat quarter.

Pouch Assembly

Refer to General Appliqué Instructions (page 17) as needed. Seam allowance is ¼″.

1. Make templates for the pouch using strawberry shapes 26–29 from the *Fruitful Market Basket* patterns (pullout page P1).
2. Draw an 8″ × 9½″ rectangle on a piece of paper. Draw horizontal and vertical centerlines on the rectangle. Refer to the appliqué placement diagram (at right) and place the templates on the paper.
3. Trace around the templates to make a pattern. The tops of the larger strawberries touch the horizontal centerline, and the strawberries should almost touch each other.
4. Make an overlay from the pattern.

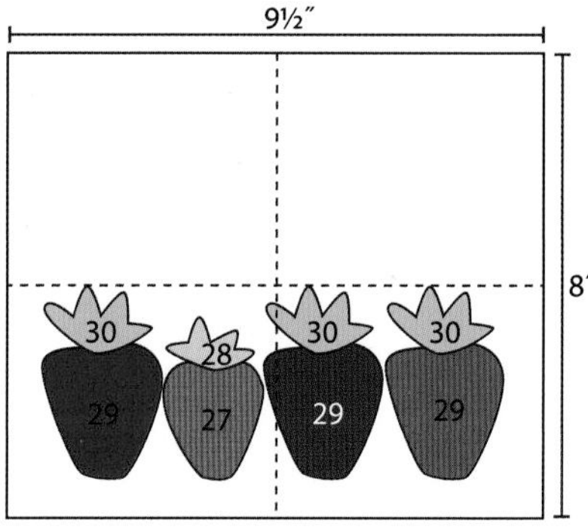

Appliqué placement

5. Press the background in half horizontally and vertically. Place it on your design wall.

6. Refer to Preparing to Stitch (page 14) to choose fabrics, fuse the fusible web to all the felted wool appliqués, and cut them out.

7. Place the appliqué pieces on the background on your design wall. Use the overlay to place the appliqué pieces in the proper position, or place them by eye. Play with color and fabric choices until you are happy with the way the block looks.

8. Fuse and appliqué the pouch front. Select your appliqué stitch from Stitches for Appliquéing with Felted Wool (page 25). Embroider straight lines through all layers for the seeds.

9. Follow the manufacturer's instructions and press the fusible web to the wrong side of the lining fabric. Fuse the lining fabric, centered, to the wrong side of the pouch front. Use a nonstick pressing sheet to protect the iron and ironing board.

Fuse lining to wrong side of pouch front.

10. Press the lined pouch front on the wrong side, and trim it to 8″ × 9½″.

Preparing the Zipper Side of the Pouch

1. Move the zipper pull down about 13″, opening the zipper.

2. Using the zipper foot on your sewing machine, sew a zipper facing strip to each side of the zipper, right sides together. Open out the facings and press.

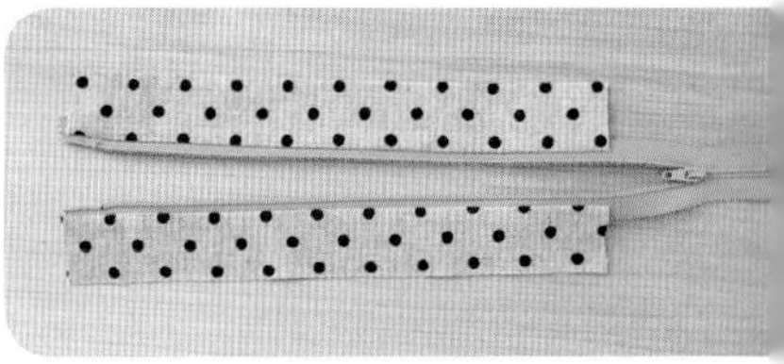

Sew and press zipper facing strip to each side of zipper.

3. Close the zipper. Trim the pull end as shown, leaving ½″ of fabric and zipper tape extending beyond the zipper pull. Measure 9½″ along the length of the zipper and trim away the excess fabric and zipper.

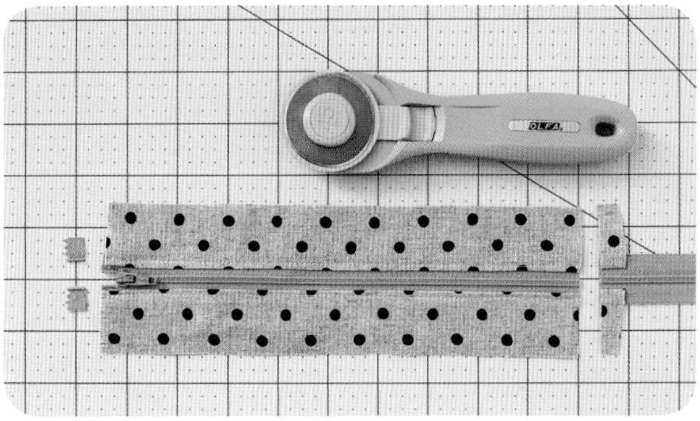

Trim excess zipper and facing.

4. Place the zipper unit right side up on a table, with the zipper pull on the right. Clip, and then sew, the clear vinyl to the zipper unit as shown.

5. Open up the seam and finger press the seam allowances toward the zipper facing.

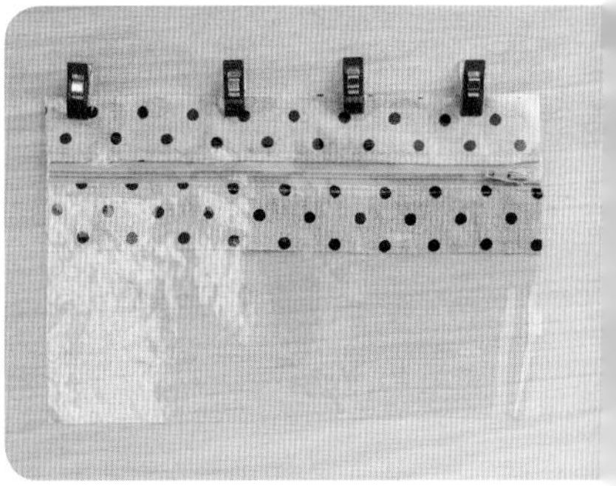

Clip and sew vinyl to zipper.

Binding Preparation

1. Trim an end of each bias strip so that both ends are at the same 45° angle.

2. Refer to the photo in Straight-Grain Binding from Strips (page 37) to place the 2 strips right sides together. Offset the ends to form a V at the ¼″ seamline. Sew the bias strips right sides together, end to end. Press the seam allowance open.

3. **If you have a bias tape maker:** Follow the instructions in this step; otherwise, go to Step 4.

Feed an end of the strip through the bias strip maker. As you move the tool down the strip, the edges are folded in toward the center of the strip, wrong sides together. Move the tool slowly and press with a hot iron as you go. If you use steam, be careful not to burn yourself.

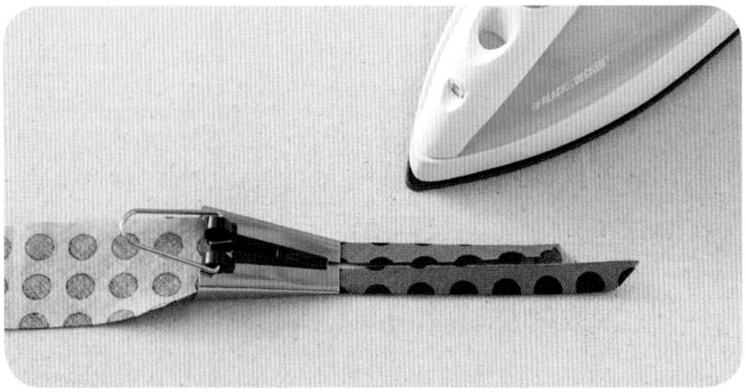

Feed bias strip through bias tape maker.

Fold the pressed bias in half, with the raw edges to the inside of the finished bias tape.

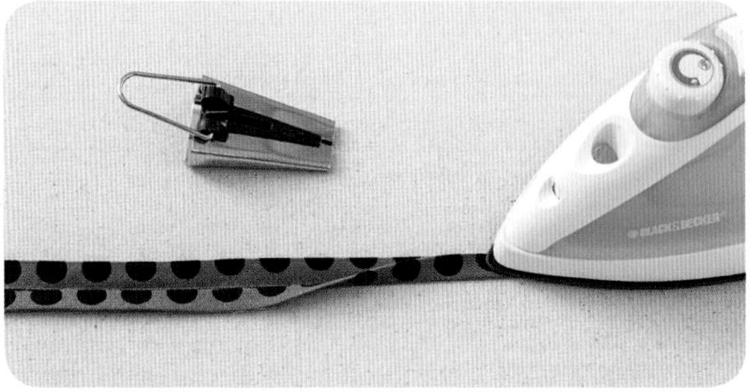

Fold bias in half.

4. **If you don't have a bias tape maker:** Fold the bias in half and press. Unfold, fold the raw edges to the fold line, and press. Fold the bias tape in half.

Clear Vinyl Sewing Tips

- If you pin through the vinyl, the pins will leave holes in the vinyl. If you don't have binding clips you can try using hair clips or a glue stick.
- It is easier to sew with the vinyl on top, not next to the feed dogs. The vinyl wants to grip the bed of the sewing machine, making it harder to sew smoothly. If you do have to sew with the vinyl side down, place tissue paper between the vinyl and the bed of the machine to keep it from sticking.
- Use a walking foot when sewing with the vinyl on top.
- Set the machine to a relatively long stitch when sewing vinyl. If you have too many stitches close together they can tear the vinyl at the seamline.

Strawberry Pouch Assembly

1. Make the corner template using the pattern (below).
2. Clip the 2 sides of the pouch with wrong sides together. Be sure that the front and back are oriented the same way, with the appliqués and the vinyl at the bottom.
3. With the zipper/vinyl side up, baste together the 4 edges of the pouch on the sewing machine with a scant ¼″ seam allowance.
4. Place the template on each corner of the pouch, lining up the edge of the circle with the raw edges at each corner. Trace around the template and cut away the excess fabric to make rounded corners.

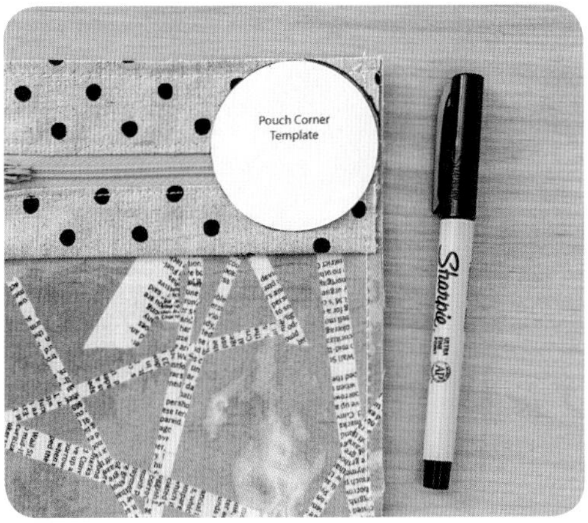

Use template to round corners.

5. Clip the binding to the edges of the pouch, encasing the raw edges as shown. Cut the bias where the ends meet straight, not at an angle, leaving ½″ of overlap. Leave the first and last few inches of the binding unclipped.

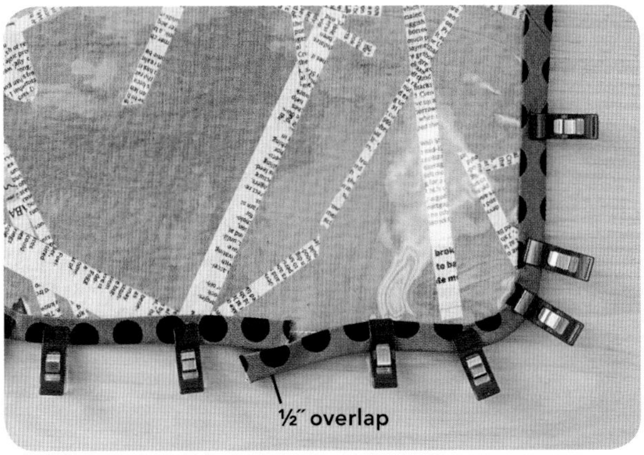

Clip binding to pouch.

6. Unfold the ends of the bias strips and pin them right sides together.

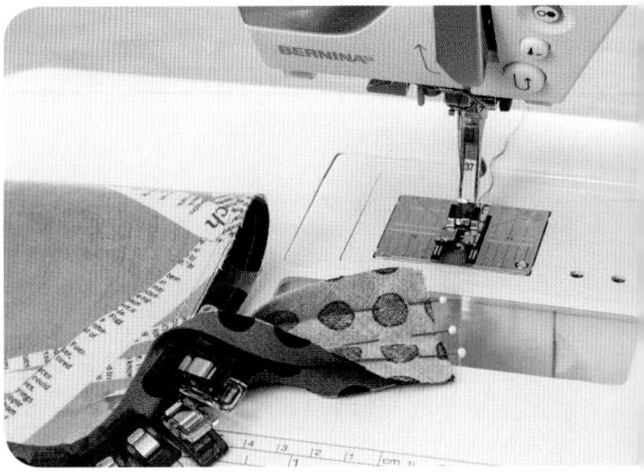

Pin together binding ends.

7. Sew together the ends. Finger-press the seam allowances open. Refold the bias strip and clip it in place, over the raw edge of the pouch.
8. Sew through all layers with thread that matches the bias strip.

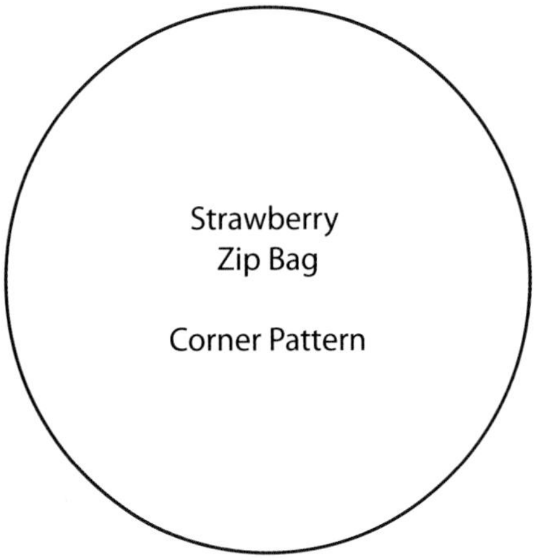

Strawberry Pincushions

FINISHED SIZES: 3″ × 3½″ and 2⅜″ × 2½″

Made by Becky Goldsmith

Of course you need a strawberry pincushion to go with the Strawberry Pouch (page 51). These strawberry pincushions are a quick, hand-sewn project. You'll want to make at least one for yourself—and then more for your friends.

By the way, these make really cute Christmas ornaments.

Materials

- Red felted wool for large strawberry: 1 scrap 3½″ × 7″ per pincushion
- Red felted wool for small strawberry: 1 scrap 3″ × 5½″ per pincushion
- Green felted wool for large topper: 1 scrap 3″ × 3¾″ per pincushion
- Green felted wool for small topper: 1 scrap 2½″ × 3″ per pincushion

Additional supplies

- Self-adhesive laminating sheets: 1 sheet
- Threads: Perle cotton size 12 in colors to match or complement the fabrics
- Ribbon: A short scrap for the stem
- Stuffing: Use lizard litter or wool, cotton, or polyester stuffing

Pincushion Assembly

Refer to General Appliqué Instructions (page 17) as needed.

1. Make templates for the pincushions using the Strawberry Pincushions patterns (pullout page P3).
2. Place the felted wool right side up on a sandpaper board. Place the template right side up on the felted wool and trace around it.
3. Cut out all the felted wool pieces.

Tracing on Felted Wool

Felted wool is fuzzy, which makes it hard to write on. You can sometimes use a chalk pencil, but if that isn't working for you, use a Sharpie Ultra Fine Point marker or something similar. Draw the line just a little bit away from the edge of the template.

When you cut away the excess fabric, be sure to cut off the drawn line.

4. Place the strawberry topper over the centerline of the strawberry, both shapes right side up. Turn the topper so that it is slightly on the diagonal. Sew the 2 shapes together with a stem stitch (page 27) to create veins.

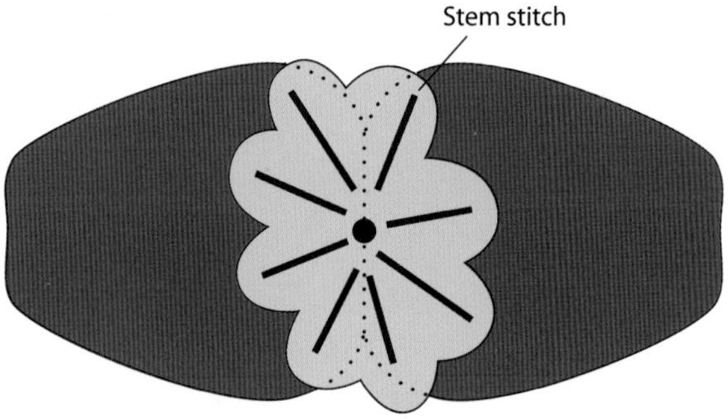

Use stem stitch to sew shapes together.

5. Cut a small slit ⅛″–³⁄₁₆″ long in the top center of the strawberry, through both pieces of felt. Pull a loop of ribbon or trim through the slit. Sew the ends of the ribbon in place on the inside of the strawberry.

   Alternate stem option: Don't cut the slit; finish the pincushion as described in Steps 6–8. Sew a special bead or button to the top of the strawberry instead of the stem.

6. Sew seeds on the strawberry. Becky used black perle cotton size 12 to sew several short lines. You could use embroidery floss, narrow silk ribbon, beads, or anything else that suits you.

Add seeds to strawberry.

7. Fold the strawberry in half, right sides together. Sew together the 2 sides with a running stitch about ⅛″ inside of the cut edges. Use doubled perle cotton size 12 or multiple strands of embroidery floss in a color to match or coordinate with the strawberry. Stop sewing about 1¼″ away from the end.

8. Stuff the strawberry as full as you want it to be. Sew the opening closed and knot the thread. Fill it with pins and enjoy using it.

Kitchen Quilts

FINISHED QUILT SIZE: 8″ × 8″

Made by Linda Jenkins

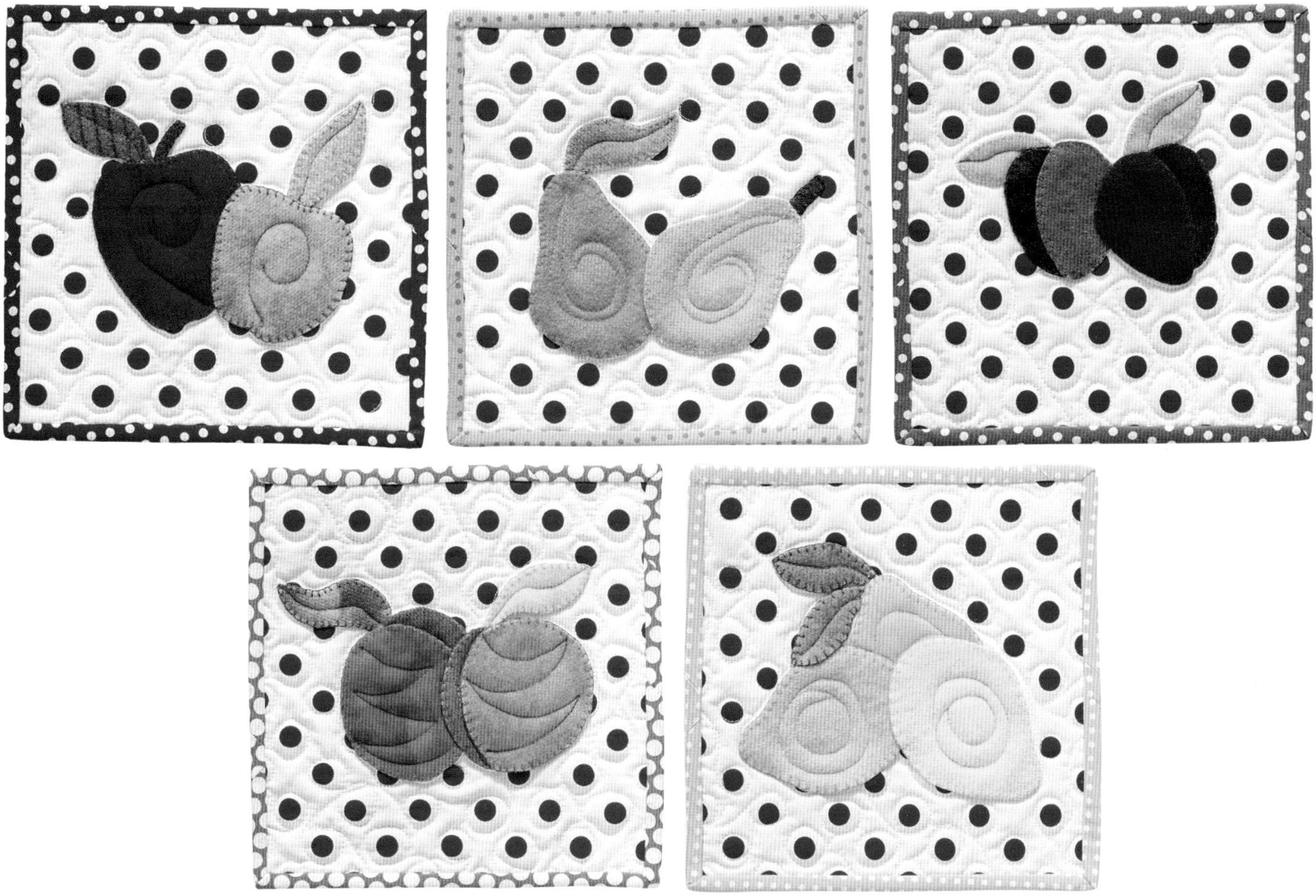

You can pick your favorite fruits from *Fruitful Market Basket* (page 48) and scatter them on small quilts, place mats, table runners, pillows, and more. Linda made these cute quilts to hang in her kitchen.

Materials

- Cotton or linen block background fabric for all blocks: ⅔ yard
- Appliqué fabrics: A variety of scraps of felted wool for the fruit
- Binding: ⅛ yard each of 5 fabrics to make 5 straight-grain bindings (see Customize the Binding, below right)
- Backing and sleeve: 1 fat quarter per quilt
- Batting: 5 squares 12″ × 12″

Additional supplies

- Self-adhesive laminating sheets: 4 sheets
- Fusible web: 4 sheets of SoftFuse *OR* ½ yard of 18″-wide fusible
- Clear vinyl: ¼ yard of 54″ wide *OR* ⅔ yard of 16″–18″ wide
- Appliqué threads: Aurifil wool in colors to match or complement the fabrics

Cutting

WOF = width of fabric

Block background fabric

Cut 5 squares 10″ × 10″.

Binding

Cut 1 strip 2½″ × WOF from each of 5 fabrics to make a straight-grain binding strip for each quilt. See Straight-Grain Binding from Strips (page 37).

Customize the Binding

These quilts are especially cute when bound with different fabrics. You can make straight-grain binding from a 2½″ × width of fabric strip to bind each quilt—this is the method described in this project.

You can also make one binding to use on all five quilts. If you do that, it makes sense to make bias binding from a square. If you want to do that, you will need ⅞ yard, to make binding from a 26″ × 26″ square.

One last option is to use scraps of binding left over from other projects.

Quilt Assembly

Refer to General Appliqué Instructions (page 17) as needed.

1. Make templates for the fruit shapes using the *Fruitful Market Basket* patterns (pullout page P1).

   Note: The shape numbers in the diagrams are the same as those in *Fruitful Market Basket*. If a shape number is followed by an R, that means that the template has been turned upside down to create a mirror image (or reverse image) of the shape.

2. Draw an 8″ × 8″ square on a piece of paper. Draw horizontal and vertical centerlines on the square. Refer to the appliqué placement diagrams (on this page) and place the templates on the paper. Trace around the templates to make a pattern. Repeat for each fruit quilt.
3. Make an overlay for each quilt from the patterns.
4. Press the backgrounds in half horizontally and vertically. Place them on your design wall.
5. Refer to Preparing to Stitch (page 14) to choose fabrics, fuse the fusible web to all the felted wool appliqués, and cut them out.
6. Place the appliqué pieces on the backgrounds on your design wall. Use the overlays to place the appliqué pieces in the proper position, or place them by eye. Play with color and fabric choices until you are happy with the way the block looks.
7. Fuse and appliqué the blocks. Select your appliqué stitch from Stitches for Appliquéing with Felted Wool (page 25).
8. When the appliqué is complete, press the blocks on the wrong side, and trim them to 8½″ × 8½″.
9. Layer and baste each quilt. Quilt by hand or machine, and bind. Refer to Finishing Techniques (page 34).

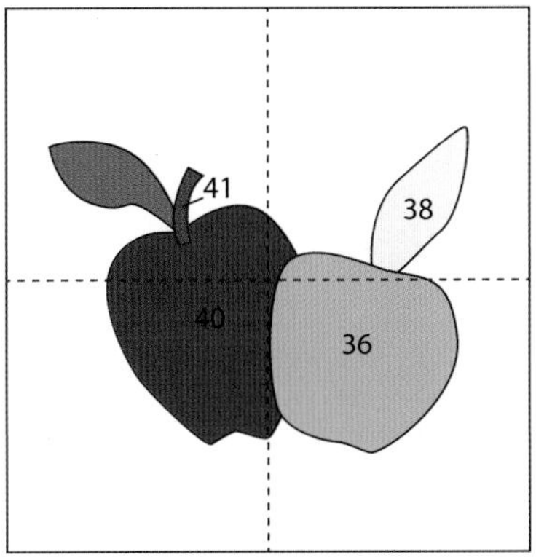

Apples appliqué placement

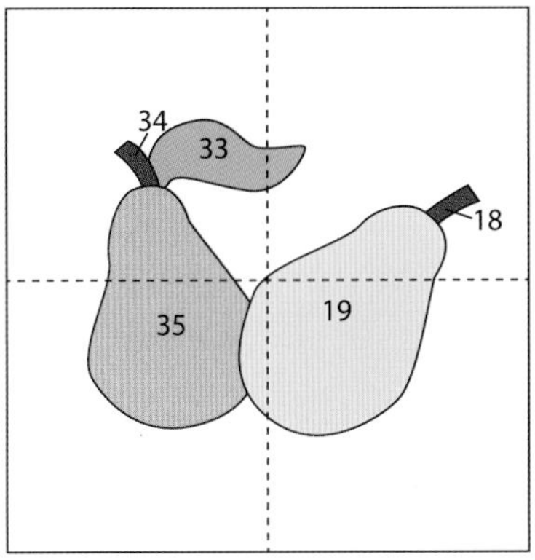

Pears appliqué placement

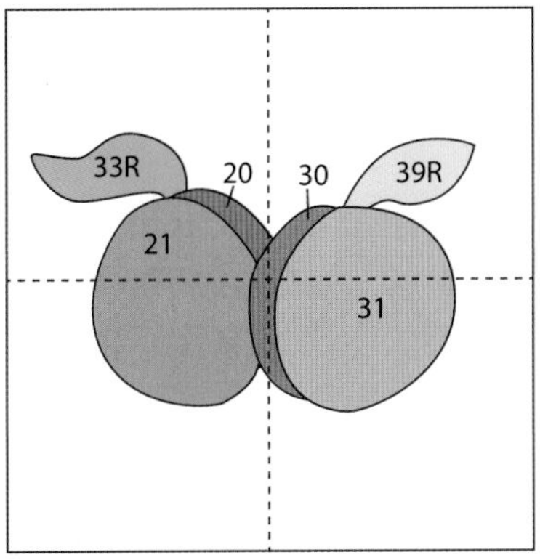

Peaches appliqué placement

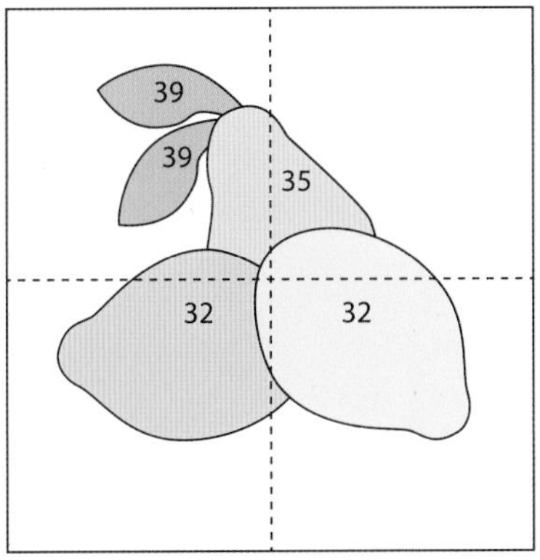

Pear and lemons appliqué placement

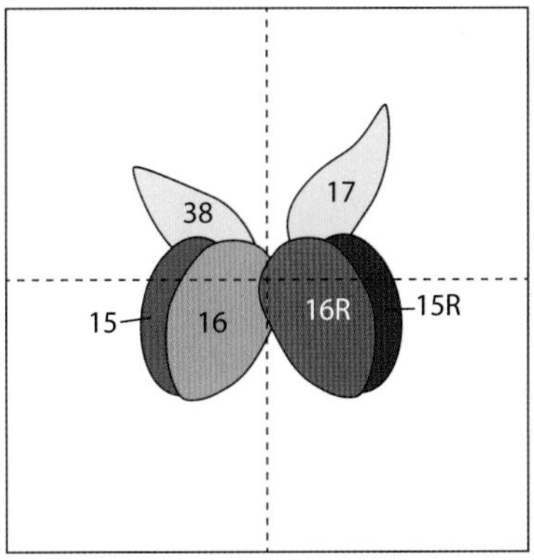

Plums appliqué placement

Leafy Pillows

FINISHED PILLOW SIZE: 18″ × 18″

Made by Linda Jenkins

These happy pillows bring a room to life and make it smile. Linda used thin-wale corduroy for her pillow backgrounds and embroidered veins on the felted wool leaves with perle cotton size 16.

Materials

(For 2 pillows)

- Pillow front fabric (corduroy): ⅔ yard
- Appliqué fabrics:

  Leaves: 6 or more different green felted wool Chunks (9″ × 10″)

  Stems: 2 greenish-yellow felted wool Chunks (9″ × 10″) or 1 Chubby (16″ × 16″)

  Circles: A scrap of a dotted cotton fabric

- Pillow back fabric: ⅔ yard
- Cotton fabric to cover piping cord: ⅔ yard

Additional supplies

- Self-adhesive laminating sheets: 6 sheets
- Clear vinyl: ⅝ yard of 54″ wide *OR* ⅝ yard of 16″–18″ wide
- Fusible web: 8 sheets of SoftFuse *OR* 1 yard of 18″-wide fusible
- Appliqué threads: Aurifil wool in colors to match or complement the fabrics
- Embroidery thread: Perle cotton size 12 or 16 for leaf veins
- ¼″ cotton cord for the piping: 4½ yards
- Polyester stuffing: 1 bag

Cutting

Block background fabric

Cut 2 squares 20″ × 20″.

Pillow back fabric

Cut 2 squares 18½″ × 18½″.

Piping

Cut 1 square 21″ × 21″ to make a 2″-wide continuous bias strip 165″ long for the piping at the edge of the pillows (see Continuous Bias Binding, page 36).

Stuffing the Pillows

Linda tried using a pillow form in her pillows, but she thought that they were too full. She chose to stuff the pillow itself and sew it closed.

After talking about it, we both realized that even though our throw pillows have removable covers and could be washed, neither of us ever does that. We treat special pillows carefully to preserve their look, but even so, throw pillows are not forever sorts of objects. We get tired of one look and trade it out for another at some point.

Stuffing the pillow with polyester stuffing is less expensive than using a pillow form, and it is easier to construct a pillow that is sewn closed, which is how these instructions are written.

If you want to, you can insert a zipper on the back in much the same way that the zipper is sewn into the Strawberry Zip Bag (page 51). To do this, cut a piece of backing fabric 20″ × 20″. Cut it apart at the point where you want the zipper to be. Sew in the zipper and then trim the pillow back to 18½″ × 18½″.

Pillow Assembly

Refer to General Appliqué Instructions (page 17) as needed.

1. Make templates and overlays for the block using the Leafy Pillows patterns (pullout page P4).

2. Press the backgrounds in half horizontally and vertically. Place them on your design wall.

3. Refer to Preparing to Stitch (page 14) to choose fabrics, fuse the fusible web to all the felted wool appliqués, and cut them out.

4. Place the appliqué pieces on the backgrounds on your design wall. Use the overlay to place the appliqué pieces in the proper position, or place them by eye. Play with color and fabric choices until you are happy with the way the pillows look.

Appliqué placement

5. Fuse and appliqué the pillows. Select your appliqué stitch from Stitches for Appliquéing with Felted Wool (page 25).

6. When the appliqué is complete, embroider the veins in the leaves using a stem stitch (page 27).

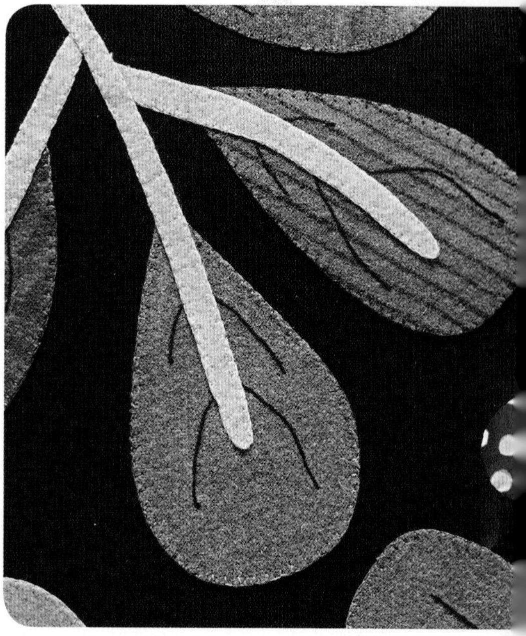

Embroider leaf veins with stem stitch.

7. Press the pillow fronts on the wrong side, and trim each to 18½″ × 18½″.

8. Refer to Piping (page 39) to make and sew the cording to the edge of the pillow tops.

9. Pin a pillow top to a pillow back, right sides together, with the piping in between. Use a zipper foot and sew together the pillow with a ¼″ seam allowance, leaving a 4″ opening in the center of a side.

10. Turn the pillows right side out. Stuff each with polyester stuffing and stitch the opening closed by hand.

Leafy Table Topper

FINISHED QUILT SIZE: 18″ × 40″

Made by Becky Goldsmith

Materials

- Cotton background fabric: ⅔ yard
- Cotton end strips and binding: ⅞ yard
- Appliqué fabrics:

  Leaves: 5 felted wool Chunks (9″ × 10″) in a variety of shades of blue

  Some leaves and blue end strips: 1 piece of felted wool that is at least 7″ × 18½″

  Stems: ¼ yard cotton fabric

  Circles: A scrap of a dotted cotton fabric
- Backing and sleeve: 1⅓ yards

Additional supplies

- Self-adhesive laminating sheets: 6 sheets
- Clear vinyl: ⅝ yard of 54″ wide *OR* 1⅛ yards of 16″–18″ wide
- Fusible web: 8 sheets of SoftFuse OR 1 yard of 18″-wide fusible
- Appliqué threads: Perle cotton size 12 *AND/OR* Aurifil wool in colors to match or complement the fabrics

Cutting

WOF = width of fabric

Block background fabric

Cut 1 rectangle 20″ × 38″ for the block background.

Cotton end strip fabric

Cut 2 strips 1½″ × 18½″.

Felted wool end strip fabric

Cut 2 strips 1½″ × 18½″.

Binding

Cut 1 square 22″ × 22″ to make a 2½″-wide continuous bias strip 130″ long for the binding (see Continuous Bias Binding, page 36).

Block Assembly

Refer to General Appliqué Instructions (page 17) as needed.

1. Make templates using the Leafy Pillows patterns (pullout page P4).
2. Draw an 18″ × 36″ rectangle on a piece of paper. (Use a wide roll of paper or tape together regular-sized pages as needed.) Draw horizontal and vertical centerlines on the rectangle.
3. Refer to the appliqué placement diagram (below) and place the templates on the paper. Trace around them to make a pattern.
4. Make an overlay from the pattern.
5. Press the background in half horizontally and vertically. Place it on your design wall.
6. Refer to Preparing to Stitch (page 14) to choose fabrics, fuse the fusible web to all the felted wool appliqués, and cut them out.
7. Place the appliqué pieces on the background on your design wall. Use the overlay to place the appliqué pieces in the proper position, or place them by eye. Play with color and fabric choices until you are happy with the way the block looks.
8. Fuse and appliqué the block. Select your appliqué stitch from Stitches for Appliquéing with Felted Wool (page 25).
9. When the appliqué is complete, press the quilt top on the wrong side, and trim it to 18½″ × 36½″.

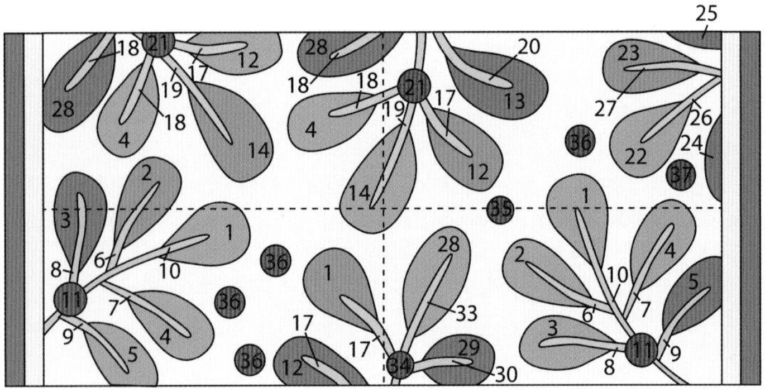

Appliqué placement and quilt assembly diagram

Quilt Assembly

Seam allowances are ¼″.

1. Sew a cotton end strip to a felted wool end strip. Press the seam allowances toward the cotton strip. Repeat for the other cotton and felted wool end strips.
2. Sew the end strips to the ends of the table topper, with the cotton strip next to the table topper. Press the seam allowances toward the cotton end strips.
3. Layer and baste the quilt. Quilt by hand or machine, and bind. Refer to Finishing Techniques (page 34).

Jamestown Avenue

FINISHED QUILT SIZE: 38″ × 8″

Made by Linda Jenkins

Linda grew up on Jamestown Avenue in Tulsa, and all of the houses on the street were different from each other. The house across the street from her sat on acreage with lots of trees. She loved seeing the leaves change color in the fall.

This small quilt is perfect to use over a doorway or on a table.

Materials

- Block background: 4 felted wool pieces in a variety of greens to make a 10″ × 40″ background
- Cotton fabric for the grass: ¼ yard
- Appliqué: A variety of felted wool scraps for houses, trees, and leaves
- Backing and sleeve: 1½ yards cotton fabric
- Binding: ⅝ yard cotton fabric
- Batting: 16″ × 46″

Additional supplies

- Self-adhesive laminating sheets: 5 sheets
- Clear vinyl: ⅓ yard of 54″ wide *OR* 1⅛ yards of 16″–18″ wide
- Fusible web: 6 sheets of SoftFuse *OR* ⅔ yard of 18″-wide fusible
- Buttons: 4 for doorknobs
- Appliqué threads: Aurifil wool for houses and perle cotton size 12 for the grass in colors to match or complement the fabrics

Cutting

WOF = width of fabric

Block background fabric

Cut felted wool in various sizes and construct a rectangle 10″ × 40″ for the block background. Use a ¼″ seam allowance. Press the seams open gently, using a pressing cloth.

The following are the sizes Linda cut and pieced together, from left to right:

8¼″ × 10″, 8½″ × 10″,
10″ × 14½″, 10″ × 10¼″

Grass fabric

Cut 1 strip 2″ × 40¾″.

Binding

Cut 1 square 20″ × 20″ to make a 2½″-wide continuous bias strip 120″ long for the binding (see Continuous Bias Binding, page 36).

Quilt Assembly

Refer to General Appliqué Instructions (page 17) as needed. Seam allowances are ¼″.

1. Make templates and overlays for the block using the *Jamestown Avenue* patterns (pullout page P2).
2. Sew together background pieces and press the seams open. Linda used felted wool, but you can use any fabric you like for the quilt.
3. A felted wool background is too thick to press in half horizontally and vertically. Instead, fold the background in half and draw a ¼″-long line at each edge of the background to mark the horizontal and vertical centerlines. Place the background on your design wall.
4. Refer to Preparing to Stitch (page 14) to choose fabrics, fuse the fusible web to all the felted wool appliqués, and cut them out.
5. Place the appliqué pieces on the background on your design wall. Use the overlay to place the appliqué pieces in the proper position, or place them by eye. Play with color and fabric choices until you are happy with the way the block looks.
6. Fuse and appliqué the block. Select your appliqué stitch from Stitches for Appliquéing with Felted Wool (page 25). Refer to Appliqué with Attitude on Cotton (page 31) to stitch the ground to the background.
7. When the appliqué is complete, embroider the insides and outsides of the windows and around the doors using a stem stitch (page 27) and wool thread.
8. Press the quilt on the wrong side, and trim it to 8½″ × 38½″.
9. Layer and baste the quilt. Quilt by hand or machine, and bind. Refer to Finishing Techniques (page 34).

Appliqué placement

Tulips Do the Polka

FINISHED BLOCK SIZE: 18″ × 18″
FINISHED QUILT SIZE: 45¾″ × 45¾″

Made by Linda Jenkins

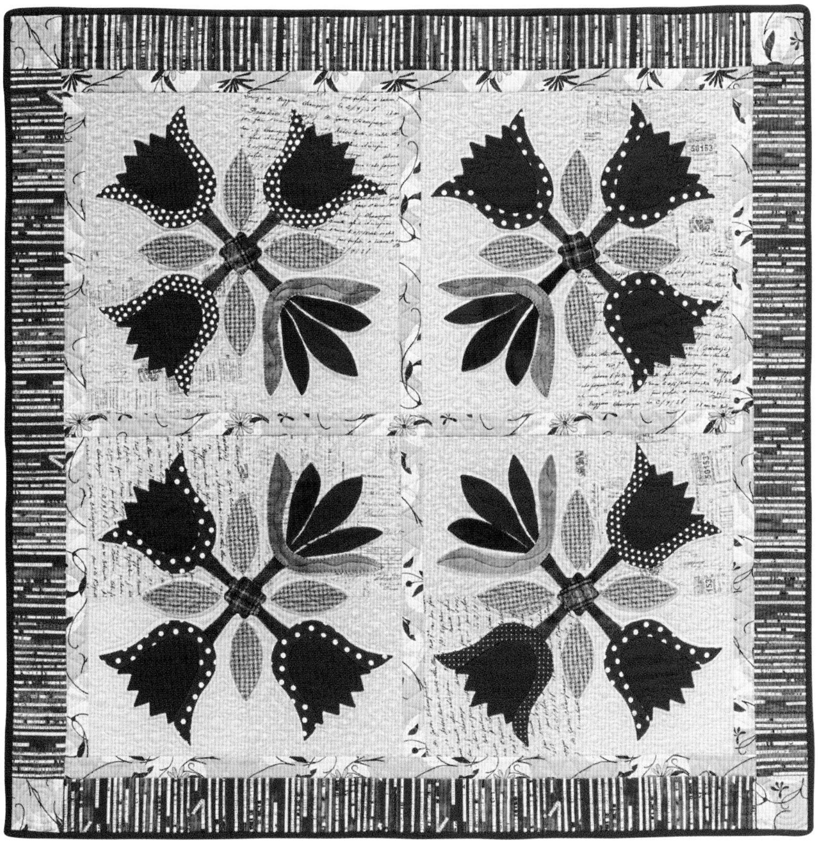

Twirling tulips cut from red felted wool dance and polka dotted cottons bring a smile to your face. This pattern would also be fun to make with only cotton prints stitched with attitude. Color the tulips as Linda did and they are perfect for Christmas, or color them to match your decor.

Look close—there is one flower in each block that is different. When four blocks are set together, these different flowers form a subtle square in the center of the quilt that the more traditional tulips dance around.

Materials

For the background, Linda used LaCouture fabric by Stof. For the sashing and corner squares, she used Gypsy Full Moon by Felicity Miller for Westminster. The borders are Collage and Newspaper Stripe by Carrie Bloomston of SUCH Designs.

- Block background fabric: 16 squares, each 10″ × 10″ *OR* 1¼ yards of 1 fabric
- Sashing and border corner squares: ½ yard
- Outer border: ½ yard
- Appliqué fabrics:

  Outside of tulips (cotton polka dots): ¼ yard each of 4 different polka dots for the traditional tulips

  Flowers and inside of tulips (red felted wool): 1 yard or 5 Chubbies (16″ × 16″)

  Calyx (green felted wool): ¼ yard or 1 Commercial Chubby (16″ × 16″)

  Leaves (green felted wool): ¼ yard or 1 Commercial Chubby (16″ × 16″)

  Block center (red plaid felted wool): A large scrap or 1 Chunk (9″ × 10″)

- Binding: ⅞ yard
- Backing and sleeve: 3⅛ yards
- Batting: 54″ × 54″

Additional supplies

- Self-adhesive laminating sheets: 2 sheets
- Clear vinyl: ½ yard of 54″ wide *OR* ⅝ yard of 16″–18″ wide
- Fusible web: 17 sheets of SoftFuse *OR* 2 yards of 18″-wide fusible
- Appliqué threads: Aurifil wool in colors to match or complement the fabrics

About Width of Fabric

It is true that most fabrics off the bolt are a bit wider than 40″, even after washing and drying. However, we don't calculate our yardage amounts for fabric that is wider than that because, if you are unlucky and your fabric is barely 40″ wide, you won't have enough and you will be unhappy. We don't want you to be unhappy.

That said, three sashing strips and the four border strips are cut 40¼″ long. We are 99 percent positive that you will be able to cut these strips from the width of the fabric without having to piece them. However, if the fabric is just a bit too short you will have enough to be able to add to the strips to get them to the proper length.

Cutting

WOF = width of fabric

Block background fabrics

Cut 16 squares 10″ × 10″ from a variety of fabrics *OR* cut 4 squares 20″ × 20″ from 1 fabric.

Sashing and border corners

See About Width of Fabric (below left).

Cut 6 strips 1¾″ × WOF.

A: Subcut 6 strips 1¾″ × 18½″.

B: Subcut 3 strips 1¾″ × 40¼″.

Cut 1 strip 3½″ × WOF. Subcut 4 squares 3½″ × 3½″ for border corners.

Border

Cut 4 strips 3½″ × 40¼″ for borders.

Binding

Cut 1 square 26″ × 26″ to make a 2½″-wide continuous bias strip 220″ long for the binding (see Continuous Bias Binding, page 36).

Block Assembly

Refer to General Appliqué Instructions (page 17) as needed.

1. Make templates and overlays for the block using the *Tulips Do the Polka* patterns (pullout page P3).

2. Place the 10″ × 10″ background squares on your design wall. Play with their placement until you are happy. Sew together the squares with a ¼″ seam allowance into Four-patch blocks. Press seam allowances in alternate directions. Place the backgrounds on your design wall.

OR, if you cut 20″ × 20″ background squares, press them in half horizontally and vertically. Place them on your design wall.

3. Refer to Preparing to Stitch (page 14) to choose fabrics, fuse the fusible web to all the felted wool appliqués, and cut them out.

4. Place the appliqué pieces on the backgrounds on your design wall. Use the overlay to place the appliqué pieces in the proper position, or place them by eye. Remember that the 3-petal tulip in each block points to the center. Play with color and fabric choices until you are happy with the way the block looks.

5. Fuse and appliqué the blocks. Select your appliqué stitch from Stitches for Appliquéing with Felted Wool (page 25).

6. When the appliqué is complete, press the blocks on the wrong side, and trim them to 18½″ × 18½″.

Appliqué placement

Quilt Assembly

Refer to the quilt assembly diagram (below) for quilt construction. Seam allowances are ¼″.

1. Place the blocks, sashing, border strips, and border corners on your design wall.

2. Refer to the quilt assembly diagram and sew the A sashing strips between the blocks in both rows and to the ends of both rows. Press the seam allowances toward the sashing.

3. Sew a B sashing strip horizontally between the 2 rows. Press the seam allowances toward the sashing.

4. Sew a B sashing strip to the top and bottom of the quilt. Press the seam allowances toward the sashing.

5. Sew the side borders to the quilt. Press the seam allowances toward the sashing.

6. Sew a corner square to each end of the top and bottom borders. Press the seam allowances toward the border corners.

7. Sew the top and bottom borders to the quilt. Press the seam allowances toward the sashing.

8. Layer and baste the quilt. Quilt by hand or machine, and bind. Refer to Finishing Techniques (page 34).

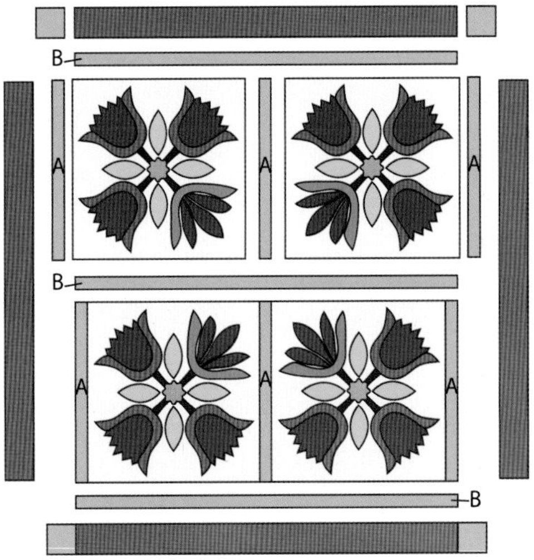

Quilt assembly

Yo-Yo Basket

FINISHED BLOCK SIZE:
14″ × 14″ or larger, depending on the size of your frame.

Made by Linda Jenkins and Mildred Phillips

Yo-yos are fun to make—in fact, they are kind of addictive. Linda's Aunt Mildred loves making them and Linda loved using them in this framed basket block.

Materials

The materials listed below are to make 1 framed block.

- Felted wool background fabric: a Chubby (16″ × 16″) or a size to fit your frame
- Appliqué fabrics: Felted wool scraps for the flowers, stems, and leaves
- Cotton prints: 57 scraps 4″ × 4″ square to make yo-yos

Additional supplies

- Self-adhesive laminating sheets: 1 sheet
- Clear vinyl: ½ yard of 54″ wide *OR* ½ yard of 16″–18″ wide
- Fusible web: 1 sheet of SoftFuse *OR* ⅛ yard of 18″-wide fusible
- Appliqué threads: Aurifil wool in colors to match or complement the felted wool fabrics
- Sewing thread: 2-ply or 3-ply regular cotton thread to tack the yo-yos to the block
- Quick Yo-Yo Maker (Small) from Clover (*optional*): This tool is very helpful in making 1¼″ (30 mm) yo-yos.
- A frame for the block
- Self-adhesive foam core mounting board to fit your frame

Cutting

Block background fabric

Measure the opening in the back side of the frame. Add 2″ to both the length and the width. Cut the background that size.

Block Assembly

Refer to General Appliqué Instructions (page 17) as needed.

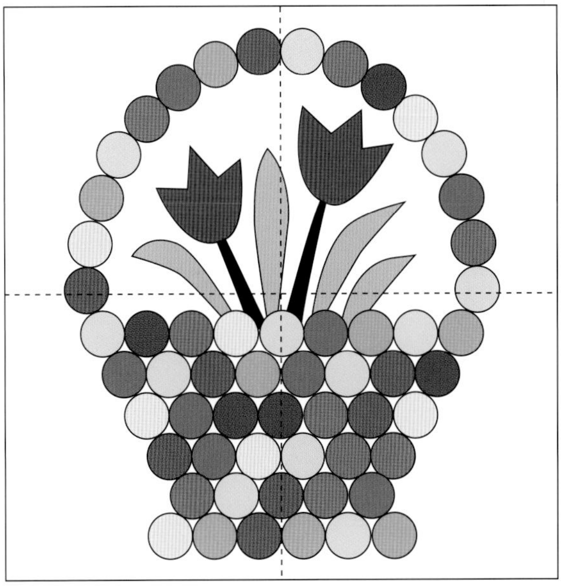

Appliqué placement

1. Make templates and overlays for the block using the *Yo-Yo Basket* pattern (pullout page P4).
2. A felted wool background is too thick to press in half horizontally and vertically. Instead, fold the background in half and draw a ¼″-long line at each edge of the background to mark the horizontal and vertical centerlines. Place the background on your design wall.
3. Refer to Preparing to Stitch (page 14) to choose fabrics, fuse the fusible web to all the felted wool appliqués, and cut them out.
4. Place the appliqué pieces on the backgrounds on your design wall. Use the overlay to place the appliqué pieces in the proper position, or place them by eye.
5. Make 57 yo-yos (see Making Yo-Yos, page 74).

Making Yo-yos

❶ If you have the yo-yo maker from Clover, follow the instructions on the package. If you do not have a yo-yo maker, make a template for a 3″ circle, using the pattern (on pullout page P3).

❷ Trace around the template on the wrong side of a yo-yo fabric scrap. Cut out the circle just inside the drawn line.

❸ Finger-press or use an iron to turn under a ¼″ seam allowance at the edge of the circle.

❹ Sew a running stitch around the folded edge of the circle with a doubled strand of regular cotton thread in a matching color. The tighter the stitch, the larger the opening in the finished yo-yo will be.

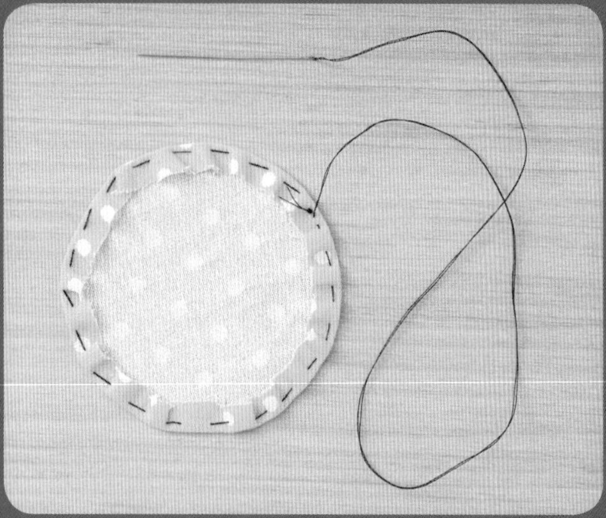

Sew running stitch around folded edge of circle; thread should match yo-yo fabric—our thread is darker so that you can see stitches.

❺ After you have sewn around the circle, pull the thread tight to gather the yo-yo.

❻ With the still-threaded needle, make a couple of tack stitches and then knot the thread. Do your best to hide the tack stitches and knot. Bury the tail of thread.

❼ Flatten the yo-yo, centering the opening.

6. Place the yo-yos with the appliqué pieces on the block on your design wall. Play with the placement of the yo-yos until you are happy with the arrangement of colors.

7. Take the block off the wall and fuse the stems, leaves, and tulips to the block.

8. The yo-yos look better if they are tacked to the felted wool background rather than being tightly appliquéd with invisible stitches. Make long stitches that catch the fabric just under the edge of the yo-yo. Since this block will be framed and not subjected to wear and tear, relatively long stitches are fine.

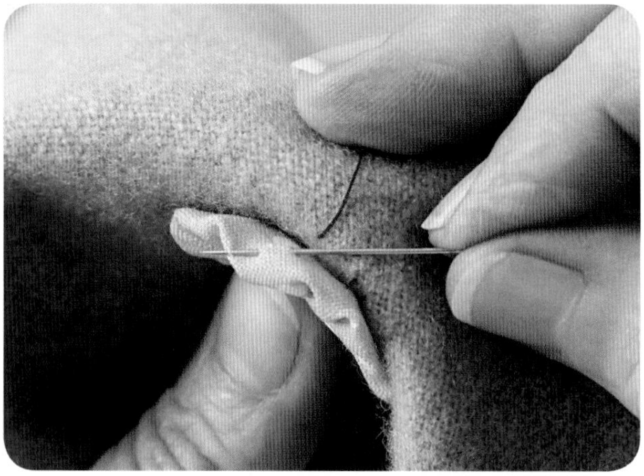

Tack yo-yos to felted wool background with long stitches hidden under edge of fabric. Thread should match yo-yo fabric—our thread is darker so that you can see stitches.

9. When the appliqué is complete, gently press the block on the wrong side if necessary. Trim the block to the size of the opening on the back of the frame.

10. Trim the self-adhesive foam core board to the size of the opening on the back of the frame. Follow the directions on the board and stick it to the back of the block.

11. Secure the mounted block inside the frame. Add hangers or wire. The shop where you bought the framing supplies may help you with these finishing details.

Vintage Gone Modern

FINISHED BLOCK SIZE: 16″ × 20″
FINISHED QUILT SIZE: 51″ × 54″

Made by Linda Jenkins

This quilt has a foot in two worlds—the traditional appliqué designs remind us of the past, while the colors and quilt structure are definitely now.

Materials

- Block background fabric: 1¼ yards
- Appliqué fabrics:

  Stems: ½ yard or 1 Chubby (16″ × 16″) of black felted wool

  Leaves: 1 dark green Chubby (16″ × 16″) of felted wool, and 1 medium and 1 light green felted wool charm square (5″ × 5″)

  Flowers and flower centers: A variety of Chunks (9″ × 10″) and Chubbies (16″ × 16″) of felted wool, and scraps of cotton prints

  Vases: 3 large scraps of cotton prints for vases and scraps of felted wool for details
- Colorful cottons for the pieced strips: A variety of fabrics to be cut into strips of varying lengths, totaling approximately ⅔ yard
- Sashing: ⅔ yard
- Border: ¾ yard
- Binding: ⅞ yard
- Backing and sleeve: 3¾ yards
- Batting: 59″ × 62″

Additional supplies

- Self-adhesive laminating sheets: 12 sheets
- Clear vinyl: ⅔ yard of 54″ wide *OR* 1¾ yards of 16″–18″ wide
- Fusible web: 18 sheets of SoftFuse *OR* 2 yards of 18″-wide fusible
- Appliqué threads: Aurifil wool and perle cotton size 12 in colors to match or complement the fabrics

Embroidered Background Fabric

Linda used an embroidered linen fabric from David Textiles for the block backgrounds. If you like the look but can't find the fabric, you can embroider your own. It's a good idea to use linen because it is heavy enough to support the weight of both the embroidery and the appliqué.

You can do the embroidery by hand or with a sewing machine loaded with heavy thread. If you embroider on the machine, be sure to use an interfacing to keep the fabric flat while you sew.

Cutting

WOF = width of fabric

Block background fabric

Cut 3 rectangles 18″ × 22″. If the fabric has a directional pattern, cut 2 tall blocks and 1 wide block.

Black cotton sashing

Cut 12 strips 1¾″ × WOF.

A: Subcut 3 strips 1½″ × 20½″.

B: Subcut 1 strip 1½″ × 16½″.

C: Subcut 3 strips 1½″ × 23½″.

Sew together the remaining strips end to end to construct the following strips:

D: Construct 3 strips 1½″ × 41½″.

E: Construct 2 strips 1½″ × 46½″.

Colorful cotton for the pieced strips

F: Cut 3 strips 3″ × 23½″

Hold the remaining fabric in reserve for now.

Border

Cut 5 strips 4½″ × WOF for the borders.

Construct 2 strips 4½″ × 43½″ for the top and bottom borders.

Construct 2 strips 4½″ × 54½″ for the side borders.

Binding

Cut 1 square 28″ × 28″ to make a 2½″-wide continuous bias strip 260″ long for the binding (see Continuous Bias Binding, page 36).

Block Assembly

Refer to General Appliqué Instructions (page 17) as needed.

1. Make templates and overlays for the blocks using the *Vintage Gone Modern* patterns (pullout pages P1, P3, and P4).
2. Press the background squares in half horizontally and vertically. Place them on your design wall.
3. Refer to Preparing to Stitch (page 14) to choose fabrics, fuse the fusible web to all the felted wool appliqués, and cut them out. Cut out the cotton appliqué, referring to Appliqué with Attitude on Cotton (page 31).
4. Place the appliqué pieces on the backgrounds on your design wall. Use the overlay to place the appliqué pieces in the proper position, or place them by eye. Play with color and fabric choices until you are happy with the way the block looks.
5. Fuse and appliqué the blocks. Select your appliqué stitch from Stitches for Appliquéing with Felted Wool (page 25) and Appliqué with Attitude on Cotton (page 31).
6. When the appliqué is complete, press the blocks on the wrong side, and trim them to 16½″ × 20½″.

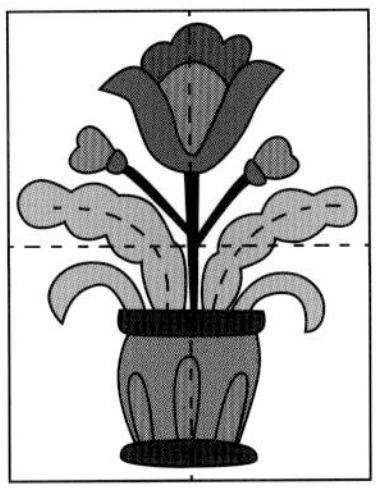

Appliqué placement—Block 1

Appliqué placement—Block 2

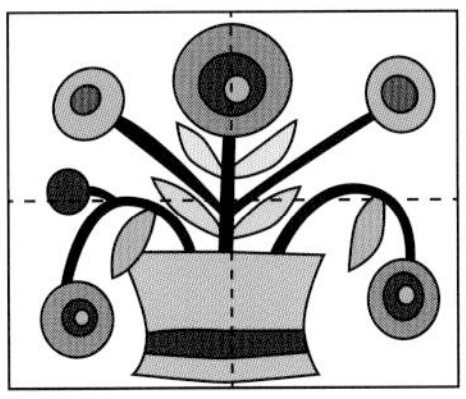

Appliqué placement—Block 3

Quilt Assembly

Refer to the quilt assembly diagram (below) for quilt construction. Seam allowances are ¼″.

1. Refer to the quilt photo (page 75) and the quilt assembly diagram (below right). Cut the reserved colorful cotton fabrics into strips of various widths. Sew colorful strips together, randomly mixing strip widths and fabric colors to make the following units:

   G: Construct 1 strip 3½″ × 20½″.

   H: Construct 1 strip 3½″ × 20½″.

   I: Construct 1 strip 2½″ × 16½″.

   J: Construct 1 strip 4½″ × 23½″.

   K: Construct 1 strip 11″ × 23½″.

2. Place the blocks, lettered units, sashing, and border strips on your design wall.
3. Referring to the quilt assembly diagram, sew an A sashing strip and H to the bottom of Block 3. Press the seam allowances toward the sashing.
4. Sew an A sashing strip to each side of G. Press the seam allowances toward the sashing.
5. Sew together the pieces in the top row. Press the seam allowances toward the sashing.
6. Sew a D sashing strip to the top and bottom of the top row. Press the seam allowances toward the sashing.
7. Sew together the F strips with a C sashing strip. Press the seam allowances toward the sashing strip.
8. Sew the B sashing strip to I. Sew B/I to the top of Block 2. Press the seam allowances toward the sashing.
9. Sew a C sashing strip to each side of J. Sew K to the C/J/C unit. Press the seam allowances toward the sashing.
10. Sew the pieces in the bottom row together. Press the seam allowances toward the sashing strips.
11. Sew a D sashing strip to the bottom of the bottom row. Press the seam allowances toward the sashing.
12. Sew the top and bottom rows together. Press the seam allowances toward the sashing.
13. Sew an E sashing strip to each side of the quilt. Press the seam allowances toward the sashing.
14. Sew the top and bottom borders to the quilt. Press the seam allowances toward the sashing.
15. Sew the side borders to the quilt. Press the seam allowances toward the sashing.
16. Layer and baste the quilt. Quilt by hand or machine, and bind. Refer to Finishing Techniques (page 34).

Quilt assembly

About the Authors

Linda Jenkins and Becky Goldsmith

The Green Country Quilter's Guild in Tulsa, Oklahoma, can be credited for bringing Linda Jenkins and Becky Goldsmith together. Their friendship developed while they worked together on many guild projects, and through a shared love for appliqué. This partnership led to the birth of Piece O' Cake Designs in 1994 and has survived Linda's moves to Pagosa Springs, Colorado; back to Tulsa in 2001; to Grand Junction, Colorado, in 2008; and, most recently, to Buckeye, Arizona. Becky headed for Sherman, Texas, in 1994 and has stayed put since then.

Linda owned and managed a beauty salon before she started quilting. Over the years she developed a fine eye for color as a hair colorist and makeup artist. Becky's degree in interior design and many art classes provided a perfect background for quilting. Linda and Becky have shown many quilts and have won numerous awards. Together they make a dynamic quilting duo, and they love to teach other quilters the joys of appliqué.

In the fall of 2002 Becky and Linda joined the C&T Publishing family, where they happily remain.

Designing and making quilts, writing books, and teaching others how to make quilts is a better career than either of them could ever have imagined. Quilters are wonderful people, and Becky and Linda love being a part of the global quilt world.

You can find them online at pieceocake.com.

Resources

C&T Publishing

ctpub.com

for the Essential Self-Adhesive Laminating Sheets, Sandboard, Appliqué Pins, and Quilter's Appliqué Caddy

Piece O' Cake Designs

pieceocake.com

for the supplies listed above as well as books, patterns, fabric, and more of our favorite appliqué supplies

Felted Wools

in the Patch designs

inthepatchdesigns.com

WoolyLady

woolylady.com

Sue Spargo

suespargo.com

Prairie Woolens

prairiewoolens.com

Other books and products from the authors

By Becky Goldsmith

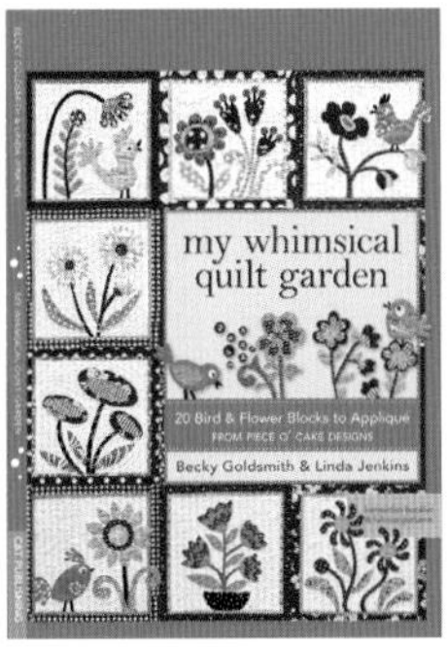

Great Titles and Products

from C&T PUBLISHING and stashBOOKS®

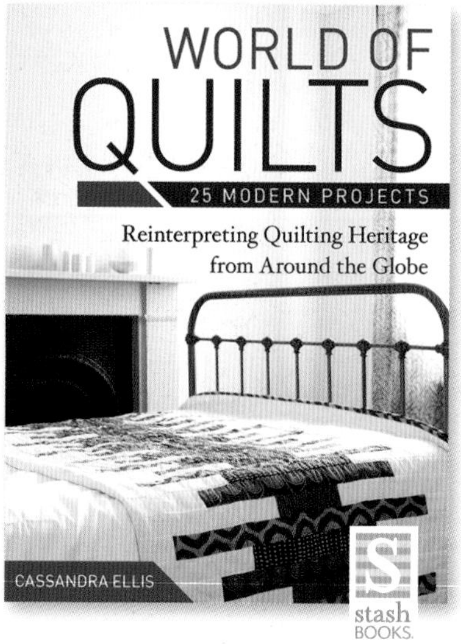

Available at your local retailer or **ctpub.com** *or* **800-284-1114**

For a list of other fine books from C&T Publishing, visit our website to view our catalog online.

C&T PUBLISHING, INC.
P.O. Box 1456
Lafayette, CA 94549
800-284-1114
Email: ctinfo@ctpub.com
Website: ctpub.com

Tips and Techniques can be found at ctpub.com/quilting-sewing-tips.

For quilting supplies:

COTTON PATCH
1025 Brown Ave.
Lafayette, CA 94549
Store: 925-284-1177
Mail order: 925-283-7883
Email: CottonPa@aol.com
Website: quiltusa.com

Note: Fabrics shown may not be currently available, as fabric manufacturers keep most fabrics in print for only a short time.